Welcome to *Reykjavik*

1

D0168026

914.912
Micheli
2019

JUN 2 5 2019

M

Colourful houses, Reykjavík
© marchello74/iStockphoto.com

Getting to Reykjavik

BY AIR

Keflavík Airport

Code KEF - ☎ 425 6000 - www.
isavia.is. Located 50 km to the west
of the capital, the Keflavíkurflugvöllur
receives **international flights.**
Compact and well thought-out,
this unique terminal offers ATMs,
currency exchange, car rental kiosks,
an Icelandair branch (☎ *p. 92*)
and a tourist office. You will find a
supermarket at the baggage claims
area and a number of boutiques and
restaurantsin the boarding area.
☺ Many return flight take off in the
early morning; it can be wise to sleep
in Keflavík where hotels offer airport
shuttles.

TRANSPORT - TOWN CENTER

Bus

Buses serve Reykjavík 35-40min after
each arrival; allow 45min journey
time. Tickets on sale in arrivals hall.
Flybus – ☎ 580 5400 - www.re.is/
flybus. Connection with Hafnarfjörður
and the BSÍ terminal (☎ *p. 95*)
or minibuses assure transfers
to accommodation. Prices: one-
way 2 950 kr, return 5 500 kr to the
BSÍ; one-way 3 950 kr, return 6 950 kr
with transfer. On your return, book
the trip to the airport the day before
through reception or the company.

Road signs
© Thorsten Henn/iStockphoto.com

Airport Direct – ☎ 497 8000 -
http://airportdirect.is. Connection to
the town centre *(skógarhlid 10)*.
Prices: from 390 kr one-way,
4 750 kr return (3 340 kr one-way
and 6 650 kr return with transfer to
accommodation).
Airport Express – ☎ 540 1313 -
http://airportexpress.is. This Gray
Line bus links the airport to the town
centre *(Holtavegi 10)*. Tarifs: 2 900 kr
one-way, 4 900 kr return (transfer to
accommodation included).

Taxi

The ride to Reykjavík costs between
13 500 and 16 000 kr and 3 000 kr for
Keflavík.

By car

A car is essential for getting to
the sites featured in this guide.
Compare prices to work out
whether it is more beneficial to
rent your vehicle at the airport or
only when you leave Reykjavík to
explore its surrounding scenery.
☛ *Cars, p. 108*.

Unmissable

Our picks for must-see sites

Gullfoss★★★ (Golden Circle)
♿ p. 63

Harpa★★★ in Reykjavík
Map D2 - ♿ p. 24

4

Seltun★
in the peninsula of
Reykjanes
♿ p. 52

National Museum of Iceland
in Reykjavík★★★
Map B5 - ♿ p. 30

Blue Lagoon★★★ in
the peninsula of
Reykjanes ♿ p. 49

Þingvellir National Park★★
(Golden Circle)
⟨ p. 56

Hallgrímskirkja★
in Reykjavík
Map D5 - ⟨ p. 27

Geysir★★ (Golden Circle)
⟨ p. 60

Lake Kleifarvatn★★ in the
peninsula of Reykjanes
⟨ p. 52

The cliffs of
Krýsuvíkurberg★ in the
peninsula of Reykjanes
⟨ p. 51

Our top picks

💜 **Savour the dream setting** and the delicate cuisine at Grillmarkadurinn, Reykjavík's most enticing restaurant. The décor is a pleasing blend of copper and metals with decorative moss, wood and local stone, with a layout that allows you to feel tucked away while enjoying a view across the two main rooms; service is impeccable. ♿ *See p. 71.*

💜 **Get a shot of history** by sitting down with Icelanders from the older generation, who often have extensive knowledge of their country. You'll only need to spend a little time hanging out in cafés to meet them: just be gentle starting conversation and you could learn a great deal. ♿ *See p. 12.*

💜 **Devour a hot dog** in the legendary Bæjerins Betzu kiosk in Reykjavik. Order a *pýlsur*, an Icelandic favourite. Here, as in many other countries, stodgy fast food has made a place for itself on the food scene. ♿ *See p. 68.*

💜 **Admire the panoramic view** from the terrace of Perlan, which dominates the capital; handy information panels provide useful detail on the landscape. You'll see the Snæfellsjökull glacier to the north and the Keilir volcano to the south, giving you plenty of inspiration to come back again for a longer visit! ♿ *See p. 32.*

💜 **Party in Reykjavík** during *rúntur*, or bar tour/crawl; it occurs at end of every week and provides plenty of festive ambiance. A drink in your

💜 **Contemplate the aurora borealis** between mid-September and the end of March. This astounding phenomenon can even be witnessed without leaving the capital, around Lake Tjörnin. Naturally , it is even better enjoyed from a body of warm water (just in case you want to make it even more magical). ♿ *See p. 20.*

© Ragnar Th Sigurdsson@arctic-images.com/Promote Iceland

Aurora Borealis over Álftanes

© Marcin_Kadziolka/iStockphoto.com

7

Bæjerins Betzu kiosk

hand and music in your ears, you'll be hard-pressed not to get swept up in the spirit of this cultural institution! ♿ See p. 25.

💜 **Relive Icelandic traditions** at the Árbær Open Air Museum. In this rural-urban space, you'll learn about historic trades and crafts and traditional daily life. ♿ See p. 38.

💜 **Hop on a bike and discover** Videy Island where you'll pass delights including an old stone farm, a basalt column, and a pebble beach. A pocket-handkerchief-sized tip of Iceland . ♿ See p. 35.

💜 **Visit the moving and isolated Strandarkirkja church** with its light-bathed, sky-blue interior and its starred volt. A reassuring and protective sanctuary for when the elements let themselves loose on this narrow band of earth. ♿ See p. 53.

💜 **Devour a Nordic thriller** by Arnaldur Indriðason then set out on the trail of his famous inspector Erlendur. Visitors love the unfamiliar and sometimes eerie atmospheric feel of Icelandic landscapes. ♿ See p. 53.

💜 **Put every second of your trip to good use** by going straight to the extraordinary Blue Lagoon as soon as you leave Keflavík airport. Prepare to marvel at the colour of the water and drift away in the 38 °C bath. Thoroughly unforgettable. ♿ See p. 49.

Reykjavik and around in 3 days

DAY 1

▶ **Morning**

Start your day in **Reykjavík★★** (p. 14) with the **National Museum of Iceland ★★★** (p. 29), the perfect place to explore the country's history via thousand of objects and photographs. Then head to **Lake Tjörnin★** (p. 20), frequented by various species of bird, before coming to the colourful roads of the **historic heart** (p. 14) of the city. Seek out a café for lunch.

▶ **Afternoon**

If you feel like making some judicious purchases, the many boutiques along Bankastræti and Laugavergur have something to suit every taste. Head north and stroll along **Sæbraut★** (p. 32), taking in the view of the sea and Mount Esja. You'll naturally come to the unavoidable **Harpa★★★** (p. 24). Be sure to get some photos of the

Kid-friendly Reykjavik

For culture, head to the National Museum (p. 29) or Saga Museum (p. 22) where your children can walk in the footsteps of Vikings. For nature, little ones will delight in watching whales in real life at (p. 100) Whales of Iceland (p. 24); and be sure to take a dip in Laugardalslaug pool (p. 33)!

architectural emblem of Reykjavík. If you have a little time left, have a peek at the contemporary art exhibitions of the **Reykjavik Art Museum** (p. 21).

▶ **Evening**

It's time to take the vibrant pulse of the city. After a drink or a meal in a café, keep the night going in **Reykjavík 101** (p. 25), around Laugavegur and Austurstræti. There will be no shortage of music, or alcohol

DAY 2

▶ **Morning**

Recover from the revelries of the night before and get out in Icelandic nature. Take Route 36 in the direction of the **Golden Circle★★** (p. 54). After about 40km/25mi, walk in the fault of the **Þingvellir National Park★★** (p. 56) to experience the movement of tectonic plates first-hand. Next bathe in the warm waters of **Laugarvatn★** (p. 59) before having lunch onsite.

▶ **Afternoon**

Head further east to **Geysir★★** (p. 60) where you can see every aspect of Iceland's geothermal activity, including the famous geysers. Follow the route (15 km/9,3mi) and prepare

© Ragnar Th. Sigurdsson/age fotostock

Secret Lagoon near the village of Fluðir

for a visual and auditory feast in front of **Gullfoss★★★** *(p. 63)*, the golden waterfall.

▶ *Evening*

Steal south via Route 30 and head for Fluðir, where you will find eating and sleeping options and can bathe in the inevitable pool for a well-deserved moment of relaxation.

DAY 3

▶ *Morning*

Head along the s**outh coast of Reykjanes★★** *(p. 52)* via Route 427. Just in case you needed proof, the vast field of lava will confirm that you are indeed on volcanic ground! In the

harbour environs of **Grindavik** *(p. 50) (which some love and some find less interesting)*, visit the informative **Saltfish Museum★** *(p. 50)* then stop for lunch in a café around the port and soak in the atmosphere at this fishing port.

▶ *Afternoon*

It's time for one of Iceland's icons: the **Blue Lagoon★★★** *(p. 49)*: surreal atmosphere guaranteed! Add to the natural delights with a massage or a spa visit. A last photo from the *platform view* and then head in the direction of Keflavík Airport, which is just 20min from here.

Discovering Reykjavik

11

Reykjavík
© powerofforever/iStockphoto.com

Iceland today

Located in the North Atlantic on the edge of the Arctic Circle, Iceland —103,125 km²), with its 338,000 plus inhabitants, 200,000 of which are in and around **Reykjavík**—has one of the lowest levels of population density in the world. Visitor numbers have been rising exponentially, with 2.2 million tourists in 2017! Iceland may be small but the country knows how to make its mark on the rest of the world: Björk made it cool in the 90s; the eruption of Eyjafjöll brought European airspace to a standstill in 2010; Icelandic footballers defied all expectations to reach the quarter finals of Euro 2016, and in the middle of the 2000s, Iceland landed at the top of global rankings for quality of life.

A well-anchored identity

Icelandic identity is composed of many ingredients: an isolated location; Viking roots; the memory of a golden medieval age; a long fight for independence and a unique language and geography, as well as a privileged (and sometimes conflictual) relationship with nature. However, though Icelanders have managed to preserve and maintain their particularities, they have also innovated across social, political, cultural and economic domains. Iceland today is a courageous, innovative place, proud of its egalitarian society and attached to the idea of collective responsibility.

Controlled tremors

The country's economy saw radical transformation in the 20C. Fishing, tourism and finance replaced agriculture, but then the financial crisis of 2008 and the mirage of virtual money plunged Iceland—a country that until this point had enjoyed audacious prosperity— into profound difficulty. Today the weakened but optimistic Iceland is back on course. Hope has been placed on new sources of growth, like tourism and energy. There remains a debate around the balance between economic interest and ecological consciousness when it comes to the management of hydroelectric and geothermal energy, but Iceland is classed as one of the cleanest countries in the world.

Journey to the center of the Earth

Iceland is an entirely volcanic island, making it a veritable geologist's paradise and anyone with a taste for nature at its most awe-inspiring. A trip to Iceland offers the opportunity to take an open-air walk on the ocean floor, be transported to Mars, or see continental drift in real-time, to witness geysers, to visit tunnels of lava and to bathe in natural thermal spas. The **Reykjanes Peninsula** and the **Golden Circle** alone are treasure troves of natural Icelandic marvels!

© Ragnar Th Sigurdsson@arctic-images.com/Promote Iceland

Austurvöllur Square with Christmas lighting

A tourist hotspot

Tourism took off in Iceland in the 80s and in the last five years has skyrocketed. It began with European hiking enthusiasts, enthralled by the fantastical Icelandic landscapes, who were succeeded in the 90s by a new kind of tourist who descended on the design hotels and cloudy waters of the **Blue Lagoon**. Today, tourism—now an essential sector of the economy—is also in recent years a source of disquiet for defenders of the environment. The number of hotels continues to increase, agencies are flourishing, farms are transforming into guesthouses and municipalities are renewing their heritage architecture. In **Reykjavik**, solo city travelers soak in the wintry atmosphere that makes the city so endlessly fascinating to thriller authors. Others may appreciate the work of architects who have gifted the capital with cafés, design hotels and luxurious villas, as well as **Harpa**, the opera house finished in 2011. If the island of volcanoes is visited first and foremost for its grand landscapes, its capital should not be neglected. You'll leave won over not only by Iceland, but by Icelanders too.

Reykjavik★★

Bathed, or even blessed, by the Gulf Stream, the most northern capital in the world has in recent years become the hottest city to visit. Minuscule on a world scale but enormous within the country, Reykjavik constitutes (almost) all of "human" Iceland. Under a vast sky, the colorful heart of the city, composed of corrugated-iron-fronted houses, inspires artists and invites visitors to snap photos. Its architectural heritage, still young but already lovingly preserved, is added to each decade by often audacious new constructions. Add to this the constant proximity of water and bird life, a rich cultural life, cozy cafés and eclectic museums—as well as the party fever that sweeps over the quiet city every weekend—and Reykjavik can count on its travel magnetism for some time to come.

▶**Access:** By bus, taxi or car from the airport (🕭 *p. 3*).
Area map: *Maps I and II p. 16-17, 19.* Detachable map
▶**Tips:** The Arbaer Open Air Museum is really worth a visit; note that outside of summer it is only open from 1pm. If you hope to see the Aurora Borealis without leaving the city, head to the edge of Lake Tjörnin, the least lit spot in town.
🛈 **Tourist Information Center** – *City Hall, Tjarnargata 11 - ✆ 411 6040 - www.visitreykjavik.is - daily 8am-8pm. 🕭 Tourist information p. 98.*

THE OLD CITY

The historic heart of the city stretches between the sea and Lake Tjörnin, to the place where the first settlers established a base. Here, you'll find a mix of cultural institutions, cafés and shops. Expect a mismatch of colorful buildings and a compact, navigable little spread of streets. Concrete, rock, corrugated iron, wood, statues and plenty of birds: surprises await you at every turn.

AUSTURVÖLLUR

C3 Austurvöllur Square was part of the farmland belonging to first settler **Ingólfur Arnarson**. A sheep pasture for centuries, today this is the heart of the capital, where people gather to work, have fun, pose and protest. Sunbathers recline on the central lawns. Political and religious powers sit side by side.

Dómkirkjan – *Mon-Fri 10am-4pm.* Constructed by the Danish in 1796 (modified in 1847) in order to mark the historical dioceses of Skálholt and Hólar, this little cathedral's charm lies in its surprisingly compact proportions. Don't miss the wood interior, warm and embellished with understated gold touches. The church faces the Alþing.

Alþing – Founded in 930 in Þingvellir, the first parliament in the world was established in this austere grey basalt edifice, topped with a copper roof,

14

Lake Tjörnin in summer

WHALES OF ICELAND

SELTJARNARNES

Northern Lights Center

Saga Museum

Grandagarður

14

Maritime Museum

Rastargata

Ægisgarður

Port

Faxagarður

HARPA

5
4

See Map II

Ánanaust

Mýrargata

Nýlendugata

Vesturgata

Ránargata

Bárugata

10

16

12

Seljavegur

Framnesvegur

Öldugata

Brekkustígur

Vesturvallagata

Bræðraborgarstígur

Hávallagata

Ásvallagata

Hringbraut

Grandavegur

Öldugata

LANDAKOTSSPÍTALI

Túngata

LANDAKOTSKIRKJA

Ægisgata

Geirsgata

Kalkofnsvegur

Hafnarhús-Reykjavik Museum of Art

Arnarhóll

Ingólfsstræti

Sólvallagata

Ásvallagata

Hringbraut

Ljósvallagata

Hávallagata

Garðastræti

Austurvöllur

Lækjargata

City Hall

7

Dómkirkjan

Bergstaðastræti

Hofsvallagata

Grenimelur

Reynimelur

Víðimelur

Suðurgata Cemetery

Suðurgata

Tjarnargata

Fríkirkjuvegur

Fríkirkjan

Skálholtsstígur

Óðinsgata

Freyjugata

Hagamelur

Furumelur

Melhagi

Birkimelur

Espimelur

Tjörnin

Skothúsvegur

Laufásvegur

National Gallery of Iceland

9

Baldursgata

18

Vatnsstígur

6

Neshagi

NESKIRKJA

NATIONAL MUSEUM OF ICELAND

Guðbrandsgata

Bjarkargata

Fjólugata

Sóleyjargata

Bragagata

Njarðargata

Fjölnisvegur

Bergstaðavegur

Laufásvegur

Fornhagi

Brynjólfsgata

8

University of Iceland

Dunhagi

U

Suðurgata

Sæmundargata

Hjarðarhagi

Fálkagata

U

Árni Magnusson Institute

Sturlugata

The Nordic House

HLJÓMSKÁLAGARÐUR

Hringbraut

Njarðargata

Smáragata

Gamla Hringbraut

Vatnsmýrarvegur

5

BSÍ

Hringbraut

Aragata

Oddagata

Tómasarhagi

Lynghagi

U

Sturlugata

REYKJAVÍKURFLUGVÖLLUR

DOMESTIC TERMINAL

NAUTHÓLSVÍK BEACH

16

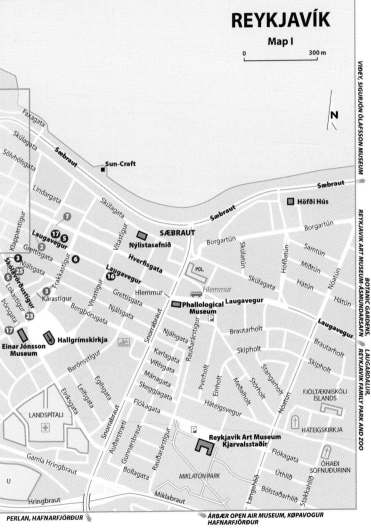

REYKJAVÍK

Map I

0 300 m

N

Faxagata

Skúlagata

Sölvhólsgata

Sæbraut

Lindargata

■ Sun-Craft

Skúlagata

Sæbraut

Sæbraut

■ Höfði Hús

Klapparstígur

⑦

⑰ ⑤ Laugavegur

② Grettisgata

③

⑤

⑮ Skólavörðustígur

Njálsgata

Frakkastígur

Vitastígur

⑥

Hverfisgata

Laugavegur

⑯

Nýlistasafnið

SÆBRAUT

Borgartún

Borgartún

Skúlatún

POL

Samtún

Miðtún

Nóatún

Höfðatún

⑤ Lokastígur

③ Kárastígur

Vitastígur

Grettisgata

Hlemmur

Hlemmur

🚌

Laugavegur

Skúlagata

Hátún

Hátún

Laugavegur

⑰

② Þórsgata

Einar Jónsson Museum

Bergþórugata

Njálsgata

Snorrabraut

Phallological Museum

P

Njálsgata

Brautarholt

Laugavegur

🏛 Hallgrímskirkja

Barónsstígur

Karlagata

Vífilsgata

Mánagata

Skeggjagata

Flókagata

Rauðarárstígur

Brautarholt

Skipholt

Skipholt

Þverholt

Einholt

Meðalholt

Stórholt

Stangarholt

Nóatún

FJÖLTÆKNISKÓLI ÍSLANDS

Eiríksgata

Leifsgata

Eiríksgata

LANDSPÍTALI ✚

Háteigsvegur

HÁTEIGSKIRKJA

Snorrabraut

Auðarstræti

Gunnarsbraut

Rauðarárstígur

P

Reykjavik Art Museum Kjarvalsstaðir

Flókagata

ÓHÁÐI SÖFNUÐURINN

Gamla Hringbraut

U

Hringbraut

MIKLATÚN PARK

Bollagata

Miklabraut

Lönguhlíð

Bólstaðarhlíð

Úthlíð

Stakkahlíð

ÁRBÆR OPEN AIR MUSEUM, KØPAVOGUR
HAFNARFJÖRÐUR

VIÐEY, SIGURJÓN ÓLAFSSON MUSEUM

REYKJAVIK ART MUSEUM–ÁSMUNDARSAFN

17

BOTANIC GARDENS,
LAUGARDALUR,
REYKJAVIK FAMILY PARK AND ZOO

erected in 1881. Today it is flanked by an altogether brighter annex (2002). The debates, which are held in a sky-blue principal room, are broadcast live. In the center of the square, the statue of **Jón Sigurðsson**, who led the fight for independence in the 19ᶜ. takes pride of place; his birth-date, June 17, is now the date of Iceland's national festival. On the east side, the white Art Deco facade of Hotel Borg, the country's first luxury hotel, embellishes the area.
Lined with some fine buildings, including the post office, and punctuated with various "historical" cafés, such as Hressó and Café Paris, **Austurstræti** connects to Ingólfstorg.

INGÓLFSTORG

C3 The old town's other square is dominated by the not particularly attractive *Morgunblaðið* building, the first daily newspaper in Iceland. Amid smoking log fires and the inevitable *pýlsur* (hot dog, 👍 *p. 120*) stands, you'll see skateboarders doing tricks and retirees taking dance classes. The city's oldest houses are mere steps away.

To the north, the roof of **Fálkahús**, or the Falcon House (1888), is topped with a longboat and four proud birds of prey. It served as a sort of warehouse for Icelandic falcons, once a good sold to the European aristocracy.
Around the square, you'll find various semi-pedestrianized roads, including Hafnarstræti and Vesturgata, replete with shops and restaurants.
Aðalstræti, or Main Street, was once lined with workshops installed by **Skúli Magnússon**, the first Icelandic governor, whose eminent role is exemplified in the statue found here. At no. 10 Aðalstræti, you'll find the crown jewels of the capital's houses. It was constructed in 1764 on the remains of a weaving workshop.
Reykjavik 871+/-2 – The Settlement Exhibition★ *C3* – *Aðalstræti 16 - ✆ 411 6370 - http://borgarsogusafn.is - 9am-6pm - 1650 kr (audioguide included).* This educational site comprises the vestiges of a farm dating from 930 and a wall face from 871, excavated during building works in 2001. Here you'll discover the history of the peopling of Reykjavik. Two paces from here, between

18

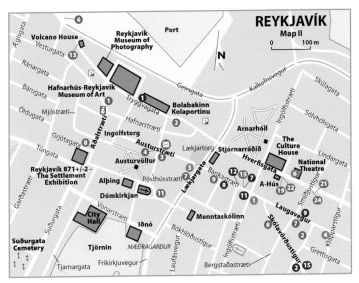

REYKJAVÍK

Map II

0   100 m

N

Volcano House
Vesturgata

Reykjavik Museum of Photography

Port

Hafnarhús-Reykjavik Museum of Art

Bolabakinn Kolaportinu

Arnarhóll

The Culture House

Ingólfstorg

Austurstræti

Lækjartorg   **Stjórnarráðið**

Hverfisgata

National Theatre

Reykjavík 871+/-2 - The Settlement Exhibition

Austurvöllur

Alþing

Pósthússtræti

Bankastræti

A-Hús

Dómkirkjan

City Hall

Iðnó

Menntaskólinn

Laugavegur

Suðurgata Cemetery

Tjörnin

MÆÐRAGARÐUR

Bergstaðastræti

Kirkjustræti and Vonarstræti, the excavation work continues.

Hidden by the *Morgunblaðið* building, delightful **little roads★** lined with colorful houses in corrugated iron climb the hill. Take Mjóstræti or Grjótagata to discover these charming floral-flanked residences, each equipped with a friendly cat. The area spreads out to the west along quiet roads, such as Ránargata. Túngata leads to the French Embassy and the **Catholic Church** (Landakotskirkja, 1929, *A1*), with its impressive neo-Gothic clock-tower.

AROUND LAKE TJÖRNIN★

C4 The **"little lake"** could be likened to an eye on the map of Reykjavik. Crucially, it allows city dwellers to stay in touch with the country's nature. It's small in terms of surface area, totally iced over in winter and domestic flights pass over it, but it is still visited by around 40 species of **birds**. You'll find children joyfully feeding them while their parents stroll the pleasant path that runs around the edge. On the north side, where birds gather waiting to be fed, are a number of impressive wood buildings, such as **Iðnó Theatre**(1891), topped with a clock tower; this was the site of the first film projection in Iceland.

Town Hall★ (Ráðhús) *C4* – *Tjarnargata 11 - ℘ 411 1111 - Mon-Fri 8am-4.15pm - free.* Since the 90s, this building has been dipping its pillars in the water of the lake. Though it's now accepted as a resounding architectural success, its placement was long contested. The building mixes concrete and glass, running water and a vertical garden. It's worth visiting just to take in the immense **map of Iceland in relief★★**. It's also a great spot from which to appreciate the formidable geography of this country and plan your upcoming walks.

On the west side of the lake, on the hillside, a little grove hides the **cemetery of Suðurgata** (Kirkjugarður, 1838, *B4*) with its tightly interlaced trees and gravestones. One headstone engraved with a phrase from Pierre Loti pays homage to French fishermen. In the charming surrounding area you'll find grand homes and typically Scandinavian communal housing.

National Gallery of Iceland★ (Listasafn Íslands) *C4* – *Fríkirkjuvegur 7 - ℘ 515 9600 - www.listasafn.is - daily except Mon 11am-5pm - 1500 kr.* On the east side, the National Gallery is housed in l'Íshúsið, a warehouse where the ice from the lake was once stored to conserve fish. The museum allows the visitor to absorb in a few short steps a large cross-section of Icelandic panting and sculpture from the 19C and 20C (Jónsson, Kjarval, Friðjónsson, etc.). The permanent collection, established in 1884, is presented on a rotating basis.

Fríkirkjan Church (1899), originally constructed using driftwood, flanks the small complex. From Fríkirkjan, the road **Skálholtsstígur** takes in a striking multicolored house and its impressive dome, ending up in the area surrounding Hallgrímskirkja (♿ *p. 28*).

HÖFN PORT

Though the grand planning projects in this area were significantly slowed by the devastating effects of the financial crisis, the port nonetheless houses a complex that welcomes an ever-growing number of visitors. You'll find two museums, an audacious new hotel and little green houses containing restaurants and boutiques. Be sure to head to **Ægisgarður pier *(BC2)*,** where you'll find the kiosks of companies, organising whale watching excursions (👆 *p. 100).*
As well as the famous and much-maligned whalers' boats, visitors will also appreciate observing repairs to some of the huge boats that occupy this port. Make sure to head to the area around the **Maritime Museum *(B1)*** to get up close to the industrial boats that made the country's fortune, and take in the atmosphere of the port. The opposite end of the port is embellished by the magnificent Harpa concert hall. Every Saturday and Sunday morning, eager shoppers head to the picturesque Kolaportið, seeking out the **flea market *(C3)*** held in a vast hall (👆 *p. 78).* The periodical arrival of foreign boats—a French naval cruiser, a US Navy vessel, a research boat returning from the Pole—adds to the life of the docks. You'll find cruise boats soaking in the **Port of Sundahöfn**, to the east of the town.

HAFNARHÚS – REYKJAVIK ART MUSEUM★

(Listasafn Reykjavikur)
C3 Tryggvagata 17 - ☎ 411 6400 - http://artmuseum.is - 10am-5pm (Thu 10pm) - 1650 kr (entry valid the same day for the three Reykjavik Art Museums).
Constructed in 1933 in modernist style, this port building in exposed concrete and metal was ingeniously transformed into a museum in the early 2000s. The vast rooms welcome temporary contemporary art exhibitions and sometimes experimental installations, a great way to discover local talent. Next, contemplate the colorful works of **Erró** (alias Guðmundur Guðmunsson), the Icelandic master of collage and pop art. A visit here is pleasingly rounded off at the museum café, with its comfortable armchairs and view across the port.

REYKJAVIK MUSEUM OF PHOTOGRAPHY

(Ljósmyndasafn)
C3 Tryggvagata 15 - ☎ 411 6390 - http://borgarsogusafn.is - Mon-Thur 10am-6pm, Fri 11am-6pm, weekends 1pm-5pm - 1000 kr.
Just next to the Museum of Art, the **library** on the sixth floor houses interesting temporary exhibitions, often offering insights into the daily life of Icelanders (think "The fjords of the East in 1920", "Icelandic women", "Immigration", etc.).

VOLCANO HOUSE

C2 *Tryggvagata 11 - ℘ 555 1900 - www.volcanohouse.is - 10am-10pm - film 1990 kr.*
Projection of documentary films on the eruptions of Vestmann (1973) and Eyjafjallajökull (2010).

REYKJAVIK MARITIME MUSEUM ★

(Sjóminjasafnið)
B1 *Grandagarður 8 - ℘ 411 6300 - www.borgarsogusafn.is - 10am-5pm - 1650 kr (children free).*
👥 Located close to the docks, this museum housed in a former fish factory recounts the maritime history of Iceland. Through the collections spreads out across spaces renovated in 2018, discover the evolution of fishing material, boats and conservation techniques. You'll find a well-appointed collection of tools, scale models, photographs, maps and recreations of modest dwellings. The museum offers a rare look into the difficulties of the sea-faring professions. A map plotting the 142 shipwrecks between 1928 and 1937 illustrates the intensity of the fishing activity during this period. The collection includes some French and Belgian boats (the *Lieutenant Boyou* of Dunkerque, the *Jan Vanders* of Ostende, etc.). The visit ends aboard the **Ódinn**, a cruiser that was used in the **Cod Wars** (👤 p. 116). From here, you can see its successor, the **Thor**, which is significantly larger and more comfortable.
Around the museum you'll find former fishermen's huts and docks housing vast industrial boats; enjoy a fine view of both from the pleasant port café Kaffivagninn (👤 p. 70).
☺ Every year on the first weekend of June, the area is abuzz with activity for the **Festival of the Sea**: think boat tours, races in the port and street parties.

SAGA MUSEUM

(Sögulóðir á Islandi)
B2 *Grandagarður 2 - ℘ 511 1517 - www.sagamuseum.is - 10am-6pm - 2200 kr (children 800 kr).*
👥 The wax and silicone statues here tell, with some realism, the (sometimes violent) major episodes of the first centuries of the country. By each scene, audio *(available in six languages, headset provided)* plays automatically, offering a concentrated burst of Icelandic history. At the end of the exhibit, you also have the chance to try on period costume and play at being a Viking!

NORTHERN LIGHTS CENTER

B2 *Grandagarður 2 - ℘ 780 4500 - http://aurorareykjavik.is - 9am-9pm - 1600 kr (6-18 ans 1000 kr).*
This exhibition comprises an educational display and some not particularly riveting scientific explanations, but is worth visiting for the cinema room. Here you have the chance to watch stunning timelapse videos with the most beautiful Aurora Borealis, filmed in the country's best viewing spots. Well-chosen calming music accompanies the wondrous spectacle; a moment of relaxation and contemplation.

Reykjavik Maritime Museum Höfn

WHALES OF ICELAND

B1 Fiskislóð 23-25 - ☏ 571 0077 - http://whalesoficeland.is - 10am-5pm - 2900 kr (7-15 years 1500 kr).

👥 The dark blue lighting of this space evokes the depth of the ocean, and this is where you'll find awe-inspiring life-size reproductions of whale species, allowing you to imagine what it might be like to swim with these majestic mammals. Note that this exhibition is fairly small and the price high.

🐋 On the port, a permanent stand promotes the **defence of whales** and contests the local tradition of whale hunting in the Inuit tradition.

♿ http://icewhale.is

HARPA★★★

D2 Austurbakki 2 - ☏ 528 5050 - www.harpa.is - guided tours (30min) from mid-June to end of August daily and all hours from 10am to 5pm; rest of the year weekdays from 1pm, 3.30pm (except Tue) and 4.30pm; weekends at 1pm and 3.30pm - 1500 kr.

A site for concerts and conferences, this immense **complex**, which also houses restaurants, bars and record shops, is the jewel in Iceland's architectural and cultural crown. Reykjavik wanted its own **emblematic edifice**, like Sydney Opera House, which would look impressive and instantly recognizable on the cover of guidebooks across the world. It was achieved, but it was a long road to get there. It was financed in part by an Icelandic businessman, but building works stopped altogether with the 2008 crisis, and then began again in 2010. Though the renovation of the sea-facing side (containing a hotel and offices) that accompanied the project had been stopped, Harpa was still baptised and inaugurated in May 2011. The **national orchestra** and artists from around the world hold regular performances in the various spaces, and Harpa, thanks to its rich cultural programming, is instrumental in conferring Reykjavik its reputation as a capital on the world stage. Whether it's the first or hundredth time you see Reykjavik's architectural icon, it's always bound to enthral. Created by Danish firm **Henning Larsen Architects** and sumptuously decked-out by Dano-Icelandic designer **Ólafur Elíasson**, Harpa stimulates the imagination. Its scale-covered shell glimmers and changes with the time of day, season and weather conditions and its surface reflects the cityscape, clouds, sea and boats. Inside, your eyes will be drawn to the lava-like smooth black walls and the ceiling covered of 3D mirrors. Light is refracted, reflected and played with throughout, so that even the exposed concrete floor takes on a life. Meanwhile, the city, bay and mountains take on different aspects through the changing prisms offered by the architecture, both in light and dark. On the facade, you'll find hexagonal carvings, which gleam like precious stones.

While the rest of the city is still catching up with the construction (a hotel is planned, but its opening

© Luis Davilla/age fotostock

Harpa designed by Henning Larsen Architects with Danish-Icelandic artist Olafur Eliasson

is pushed back each year), Harpa is outsized in comparison to its surroundings, but not intimidating to approach; it is inviting to wander. Indeed its **panoramic restaurant** is considered one of the most relaxing spots in the capital, thanks to its uninterrupted views as well as its range of cocktails and bourbons.

Letting loose Nordic-style

*On Friday and Saturday evenings, between 11pm and 5am, Reykjavik 101 (the city center) goes wild for **rúntur**. Tipsy (or more than tipsy) and spending their pennies like there's no tomorrow, young (and less young) people do the rounds of the bars and cafés-turned-clubs and continue into the early hours. Around **Laugavegur** and **Austurstræti**, you'll see lines of fun-comers waiting to see the hyped DJ of the moment or to get into the latest hip address. Dance-floors spill out onto the teeming streets, while the locals' inhibitions disappear. In summer, the party goes international with the arrival of tourists, themselves more than ready to join in! In the wee hours, taxis line up to bring everyone home, from young artistic types to white collar workers and lone night owls. Once the pocket of celebrations ends, Reykjavik returns once more it its gentle rhythm.*

EAST OF THE TOWN CENTER : LAUGAVEGUR AND HALLGRÍMSKIRKJA

Along with the historic Old Town, this area forms **Reykjavik 101**, a district that has been written about, filmed, and photographed, as well as celebrated for its cafés, bohemian spirits, street art and charming shop windows.

LÆKJARGATA AND ARNARHÓLL

D3/C4 Traced on the bed of a stream that linked Lake Tjörnin and the sea, Lækjargata crosses Austurstræti (on the Austurvöllur side) and **Bankastræti** to form the modestly proportioned main crossroads of the town center. It's dominated by a series of edifies including **Stjórnarráðið**, the 18C prison that now houses the offices of the prime minister. See also **Menntaskólinn** (1846), the large cream-colored house that was once the site of the meetings of the Alþing (parliament) before the construction of the current building (👜 *p. 18*). Heading towards the Harpa port,

you'll cross the grass of **Arnarhóll**, or Eagle's Hill, topped by a **statue of Ingólfur Arnarson**.

LAUGAVEGUR

D4-H5 Bankastræti quickly turns into Laugavegur, the rectilinear **trekking route** that was historically used by locals going to wash their things in the hot springs at Laugardalur. The length of this road, now a walking route, (👜 *box below*) is dotted with cafés and shops popular with locals and tourists alike. It crosses the crossroads at **Hlemmur** and its bus station.

The Icelandic Phallological Museum (Reðasafn) **E-F5** – *Laugavegur 116 - ☏ 561 6663 - http://phallus.is - Jun-Aug: 9am-6pm; Sep-May: 10am-6pm - 1500 kr.* This museum presents a rather curious collection of mammal phalluses!

HVERFISGATA

D3/E4 This road runs parallel to Laugavegur, but is noisier because buses pass through. Still, it houses a number of beautiful facades.

Darth Vader in the place

*Or, more precisely, in the road. In 2015 the city hall of Reykjavik confirmed the results of a sizeable **online poll**. The "Better Reykjavik" initiative, launched in 2010, invited citizens of the capital to sign up for a forum and submit their ideas for the city. One of the results was the (partial) pedestrianization of the road **Laugavegur** in 2012.*

*The city's inhabitants were also asked for their suggestions for renaming one or several roads. The result was a new road name, **Svarthöfdi** (translated roughly as 'black head'), the Icelandic name for Star Wars villain Darth Vader. It is a road in the **Höfdi district**, previously named Bratthöfdi, which was chosen to welcome the Dark Side—A Boaty McBoatface moment.*

A-Hús★ *D3* – *Hverfisgata 18.*
Undoubtedly the most beautiful
example of a wood and corrugated
iron house (1906). Note its turrets
and its mounts sculpted in bone and
whale.

National Theatre (Þjóðleikhúsið)
D3 – Designed in 1950 by Guðjón
Samúelsson, the architect of
Hallgrímskirkja, the austere building
at no. 19 creates a striking contrast
with its neighbor opposite. Its shape
is inspired by an imposing rock that
you can pass on the ring road, just
before Vík (coming from Reykjavik).

**Culture house★
(Þjóðmenningarhúsið)** *D3* –
*Hverfisgata 15 - ℘ 530 2210 - www.
culturehouse.is - 10am-5pm - closed
Mon - 2000 kr.* On the facade of
this 1906 building, the mention of
"Landsbókasafn" (national library)
alludes to the past function of this
elegant edifice. Visitors are drawn
here to admire the **parchments of
Sagas and Eddas,** gathered in 1702
by Árni Magnússon for the king of
Denmark. Later sent to Copenhagen,
in part destroyed by the fire that
would ravage the city in 1728, they
were only returned between 1971
and 1997, a victory for the newly
independent Icelanders. Classed by
UNESCO and dating, according to
some, from the 13C, these treasures
of medieval literature are presented
on the ground floor, enshrouded by a
gentle light. The history and context
of their writing and fabrication are
detailed in the exhibit. Temporary
exhibitions occupy the fine rooms of
the higher levels, including the former
reading room.

HALLGRÍMSKIRKJA AND COLORFUL ROADS

D5 From Laugavegur, the sloping
road of **Skólavörðustígur** *(D4-5)*
climbs towards the capital's iconic
church. This thoroughfare lined with
boutiques and a fine library is one
of the most pleasant in the city. It
is the neck of a network of **colorful
roads★** which stretches across
the hill between Lake Tjörnin and
Laugavegur. Wander among the
polychrome corrugated- iron-covered
houses. You'll spot tiny gardens
(where locals sunbather with even
the tiniest hint of sun), improvised
terraces, as well a hodgepodge
of architecture and a sprinkling
of good restaurants; life is sweet
along Bergstaðastræt, Baldursgata,
Njálsgata and Grettisgata!
☺ The area gets lively over the
weekend, with revellers gathering in
the mural-covered courtyards and in
the legendarycafés (Kaffibarinn and
Prikið).

Hallgrímskirkja★ *D5* –
*Hallgrimstorg 1 - ℘ 510 1000 -
www.hallgrimskirkja.is - 9am-9prm
(winter 5pm) - bell tower access
1000 kr.* At the top of the hill, you'll
find the imposing statue of **Leif
Eiríksson** (1930), the "discoverer of
America", given by the United States
for the 1,000-year anniversary of the
Alþing. It guards the entrance of the
church, symbolic edifice of Reykjavik.
Perlan and Harpa may have tried
to pinch its title, but the treasured
building staves them off on postcards
and in the hearts of inhabitants. Its

name pays homage to prolific poet and reverend **Hallgrímur Pétursson** (1624-1674), who published in 1666 the *Passion Hymns*, which are still read in Icelandic churches during Lent.

Designed by Guðjón Samúelsson (1887-1950), construction of this church began in 1946. It opened in stages between 1974 and 1986, a delay that can be explained by the fact that the building works were financed entirely by the donations of parishioners. It was worth the wait: its white facade evokes the native glaciers, while its energetic curves, like spread wings, mimic the basalt columns which enclose Svartifoss, a beautiful waterfall in the south of the island. The **interior** surprises with its modest dimensions and the heightened sobriety of the décor, which leaves the sun to do most of the work. Note the formidable 25-ton organ, with its 5,275 pipes! From atop the (73m/240ft), the **view**★ over the capital is superb, replete with a mosaic of roofs and colorful house-fronts, an ever-changing port and a selection of architectural triumphs (and errors!).

Einar-Jónsson Museum★ (Listasafn Einars Jónssonar) *D5* – Eiríksgata 3 - ℘ 551 3797 - www.lej.is - daily exp Mon 10am-5pm - 1000 kr. The neighbour of the church, this museum is dedicated to the precursor of modern Icelandic sculpture. Inspired by folklore and Nordic mythology, **Einar Jónsson** (1874-1954) left a legacy of massive works, which are displayed in what was both his house and the country's first art museum (1923). Isolated by the hill at the time of its construction, this imposing building was the first to benefit from the electricity produced by geothermal energy. The plans were designed by the artist himself, meaning this edifice can be seen, in some ways, as his largest sculpture. The hall with its blue walls presents a striking contrast to the austere facade. Visitors wander the apartment of the artist on the first floor and the (free) garden, where an army of **26 bronzes** of fantastical characters can be found.

Kjarvalsstaðir – Reykjavik Art Museum (Listasafn Reykjavikur) *F6* – Flókagata 24 - ℘ 411 6420 - http://artmuseum.is - 10am-5pm - 1650 kr (entry valid on the same day for the three Art museums of Reykjavik). Often overlooked for its slightly less central location (more to the east, beyond Av. Snorrabraut), it presents the works of **Jóhannes Kjarval** (1885-1972), a fisherman turned painter thanks to the support of his seafaring companions, who clubbed together to finance his study at the Copenhagen Fine Arts school. He painted many fine representations off Icelandic landscapes.

28

SOUTH OF THE TOWN CENTER

Directly south of Lake Tjörnin stretches the campus of the University of Iceland and the very interesting National Museum.

NATIONAL MUSEUM OF ICELAND★★★

(Þjóðminjasafn Íslands)
B5 Access : bus 12 - Suðurgata 41 - ✆ 530 2200 - www.thjodminjasafn.is - *daily10am-5pm, expt Mon in winter - closed 25, 26 and 31 Dec and Jan 1 - 2000 kr (audioguide).*
👫 Special activities on offer for children, including dressing up as a Viking!

Founded in 1863 and installed in 1908 in the current Culture House (👆 *p. 26*), the museum has been housed since 1950 in this building, when a recently independent Iceland was working to repatriate its national treasures from Danish collections. With a collection of more than 2,000 *objets* and 1,000 photos across two levels, and a well thought-out exhibition layout, this museum is undoubtedly the finest in the country. Vestiges of most of Iceland's architectural heritage can be found here. The fascinating exhibits effectively and informatively take visitors on a journey back in time. It starts with the arrival of the first settlers, their day-to-day life as peasants, paganism and the presages of Christianity (800-1000); observe the bronze statuette dating from the year 1000, which could equally represent Þórr or Christ. While medieval literature was developing, the transition with the Norwegian period is illustrated by beautiful works in sculpted wood, including the door of **Valþjófsstaður church** (1200), telling the story of the The Knight and the Lion and featuring the figure of **Christ from Ufsir**, carved in birch and coming from a painted cross that is lost today. Look out too for a cross in encrusted enamel and the huge swords (that look nigh-on impossible to wield). Reform was imposed under the yoke of the Danish. The beginnings of printing (1530) allowed for the creation of the magnificent **Guðbrandur bible** in Hólar in 1584. Old beliefs would endure however, as the many historic amulets found here attest. Talented artisans worked away crafting in their isolated farms: a superb drinking horn, sculpted by Brynjólfur Jónsson and covered in scenes from the Old and New Testaments, is an example of this work (Skarð, 1598). Daily life in the 19C is illustrated by the display of **Skautbúningur costumes**, a step towards contemporary clothing, and by a beautiful recreation of a **peasant house**. Meanwhile, a blue flag with a white cross, raised in secret by Icelandic sailors, tells the story of the desire for emancipation. Objects displayed on an airport-style conveyor belt tell the story of the 20C: the vote for women (1915), independence (1944) and patriotism, urbanization, the first television, the first flag and, naturally, the first Björk album!

⊘ The museum also presents **temporary exhibitions**; a pretty souvenir shop and café are also on offer.

UNIVERSITY CAMPUS

B5-A6 Between the National Museum and the domestic airport (of which the vast grounds attest to the ambitions of the travel industry) stretches a humid zone with a generous amount of bird-life. This is where you'll find the campus of the **University of Iceland**, which brings together some 15,000 students. The hodgepodge of buildings that comprise the campus all along **Suðurgata** were built after the founding of the university in 1911. The concrete cube of the **library** (1989) stands alongside the principal arc-shaped building dating from 1940. Not far from the Saga Hotel, typical of

the 1970s, you'll find **Árni Magnússon Institute** (*www.arnastofnun.is*), the guardian of the original Eddas and Sagas.

THE NORDIC HOUSE

(Norræna húsið)
B6 Access : buses 1, 3, 6, 15 - Sæmundargata 11 - ✆ 551 7030 - *http://nordice.is* - 11am-5pm (Wed 9pm) - free.
Near university building Askja you'll find the Nordic House with its distinctive glass roof, the Nordic. Conceived in 1968 by the famous Finnish architect **Alvar Aalto** (1898-1976), it symbolizes Scandinavian cooperation. Under its understated angled roof, conferences are convened, exhibitions are held and a library is dedicated to the culture of the countries and territories whose

A consul, a ghost and a summit

*Prefabricated in Norway, the **Höfði House** was erected in 1909 on a dolerite base facing the bay in order to house Jean-Paul Brillouin, the first French consul in Reykjavik. His Norwegian wife was behind the choice of architecture. The post was created to keep a handle on the influx of French sailors in Icelandic waters (where 4,000 of them would lose their lives, according to estimates). Brillouin worked on the construction of free clinics in Reykjavik, Heimaey and Fáskrúðsfjörður and the repatriation of bodies. In a town with only 11,000 inhabitants, the house made a strong impression with its imposing size and style. However, the consul would not get to enjoy it much as he was called back to France at the start of the First World War.*

*Many notable figures would go on to occupy this house, including the poet Einar Benediktsson (1864-1940). During the Second World War, the British Embassy would be installed here and the house would welcome Churchill. The British left in 1951, bothered by the ghost of a woman named Sölborg, once condemned by Benediktsson, now a magistrate. In 1968, Reykjavik would organize conferences here. The eyes of the world would be on this building in 1986 when **Mikhaïl Gorbatchev** and **Ronald Reagan** met for a summit here that would begin the end of the Cold War.*

flags fly at the entrance. The Aalto Bistro, a restaurant presided over by Sveinn Kjartansson, is a great spot to stop for a relaxing break.

PERLAN★

***Off map by E8** – Access: bus 18 - Varmahlíð - 🕿 566 9000 - http://perlan.is - 9am-7pm - free.*
The wood-covered hill of **Öskjuhlíð** rises up to the south-east of the town center. At its summit, you'll find Perlan, a **glass dome**, which since 1991 has covered six former geothermal reservoirs where 4 million liters of water were stored at 85 °C. Visible from across the city, Perlan offers a vast terrace with a **magnificent view★** over the capital. There is also a cafeteria on site.
The **bike route** (🚲 "Cycling", p. 106) beside the sea stretches to the east towards Kópavogur via a cemetery housing the tombs of French soldiers. To the west, it continues to the pleasant **Nautholsvik Geothermal Beach** and the new campus of the (private) University of Reykjavik. From here, the 19 bus can take you back in the direction of the city center.
🚲 There's the option to take the bike route to **Seltjarnarnes**, via pretty residential areas.

SÆBRAUT AND LAUGARDALUR

This valley, the site of farms since the 9C, slopes down to the sea and gives its name to an area now dedicated to sports and leisure.

COASTAL PATH BY SÆBRAUT★

D-H3 If Laugavegur is the direct "urban" route towards Laugardalur, the area can also be reached by the coastline along Sæbraut Street (starting from Harpa). On one side you'll find a superb view over the sea and Mount Esja; on the other side you'll find the coveted residential buildings of the pre-Crisis 'nouveaux riches' and the shining tower of Höfðatorg, the heart of the Borgartún business district.
Next you'll come to **Sun Voyager★ (E3)**, an impressive sculpture by Jón Gunnar Árnason, evoking both a whale skeleton and a longboat, whose bone-beams gleam in the sunlight. Farther on, a double anchor symbolizes the Gulf Stream "linking" Florida and Iceland. Keep going and you'll find **Nýlistasafnið** *E4 (Grandagarður 20 - 🕿 551 4350 - www.nylo.is - daily except Mon 12pm-6pm, Thu 12pm-9pm - free)*, a museum dedicated to young artists, which notably houses the intriguing **Kling og Bang gallery**, where a rotating roster of temporary exhibitions are held. Nearby you'll find the **ASÍ Museum** *F4 (Listasafn ASÍ – Guðrúnartúni 1 - 🕿 535 5635 - www.listasafnasi.is - daily expt Mon1pm-5pm - free)* also dedicated to contemporary art.
Höfði Hús★ *F3 – Access: bus 4, stop:Höfðatorg. Borgartún - http://reykjavik.is - no visits inside.* Once isolated, this 'house on the cape' is now only separated from the business district by a small patch of lawn. It's well worth stopping a few minutes in

33

front of this historical house if you get the chance (♿ *p. 32*).

Sigurjón Ólafsson Museum *Off map by H2* – *Access: bus 5, stop: Sculpture Museum - Laugarnestangi 70 - ℘ 553 2906 - www.lso.is - summer: daily expt Mon 2pm-5pm; winter: weekends 2pm-5pm - 1000 kr*. Continuing on the coastline and isolated on the sea's edge, this gallery presents the busts and sculpture of the eponymous artist (1908-1982).

LAUGARDALUR

Off map by H5-6 ♙♙ Once frequented by the washerwomen of Reykjavik, the "Hot Spring Valley", where just a few decades ago you would have found horse and sheep grazing, is now an abundant green space, a paradise for **sports and leisure activities**. Here you'll find the national football stadium, ice rink, a sports center, the vast **Laugardalslaug pool**, a campsite, a historical youth hostel and a little zoo.

Ásmundarsafn – **Reykjavik Art Museum** (Listasafn Reykjavikur) – *Access: buses 2, 15, stop: Hilton - Sigtún - ℘ 411 6430 - www. artmuseum.is - May-Sept: 10am-5pm, rest of the year: 1pm-5pm - 1650 kr (entry valid the same day for the three Reykjavik Art Museums)*. The artist **Ásmundur Sveinsson** (1893-1982), native of a lost region in the west of the country, studied art in Reykjavik and then Paris. At the gates of Laugardalur, he constructed a stunning "igloo" and white pyramids, which he would live in during the 1940s. His massive sculptures (in bronze, wood or concrete)are inspired by Icelandic nature and the Sagas. Some are located outside on the lawn *(free access)* .

Reykjavik Family Park and Zoo (Fjölskyldu og Húsdýragarðurinn) – *Access : bus 2, 15, stop: Zoo & Park - Engjavegur - ℘ 411 5900 - www. mu.is - 10am-5pm (6pm in summer) - 880 kr*. ♙♙ This modest zoo is dedicated to Icelandic animals (polar fox, reindeer, mink, seal, etc.). A small but well thought out amusement park

Peripheral walks

Mount Esja – *20 km/12mi to the north of Reykjavik. Access: bus 15 from Hlemmur to Háholt, then bus 57 to Esjurætur (Mógilsa). This beautiful mountain (914 m/2998ft) rises up across from the city, on the other side of the bay. Allow two hours to reach the summit: superb view over the Reykjanes Peninsula.*

Along theElliðaár – *Access: buses 5 and 19. Known for its salmon population (which come back up it in August), which attract some fisherpeople, this short river between Lake Elliðavatn and Elliðaárvogur bay, crossing the large southern suburbs over 5 km/3mi. It is lined by parks and sports fields, punctuated by the Árbær Open Air Museum; follow its banks for a pleasant walk in the footsteps of Reykjavik's suburb-dwellers. You'll be rewarded with pretty paths, shrub groves and picnic spots and on the east side of Lake Elliðavatn.*

(carousel, sandpit, trampoline) is on offer for the littler ones.

Botanical Garden (Grasagarður) – *Laugardalur - ℰ 411 8650 - www. grasagardur.is - May-sept: 10am-10pm; Oct-Apr: 10am-3pm - free.* This is a relaxing green space near the zoo and offers an opportunity to discover Icelandic flora.

NEARBY

Map p. 36-37

Reykjavik expands year by year, stretching out into the surrounding lava fields. Urbanization has caught up with one-time hamlets, turning them into vast—and often monotone —suburbs (Breidholt, Árbæ). These suburbs tell the story of the evolution of the individual and collective habitat during the last decades. Each of these satellite communities seeks to distinguish itself and creates its own identity with a town crest, a museum and a soccer (football) or handball team. The tourist who ventures outside of the capital will find some curiosities, which may be 'minor' compared to some of the more famous sights, but are nonetheless quite interesting. You will also find some pleasant little pockets of nature to discover by foot or to be used to take a little break .

SELTJARNARNES

B1 *Access : bus 11 –*
🇮 *www.seltjarnarnes.is.*
This commune stretches out on the **peninsula** which extends from the town center of Reykjavik looking out towards the west and the open sea. Residential zones and natural spaces sit side-by-side, offering some excellent opportunities for strolls. Many walkers and cyclists make the journey from the city center to the tip of the peninsula, along the coast. At the end of the route are sixty thriving species of **bird** (Eurasian oystercatcher, eider, tern, plover, pipit). An imposing stone building, **Nesstofa**, overlooks the area, constructed in 1767 for the director of public health. Near to a cluster of old fish drying racks, an isthmus discovered at low tide gives access to the **islet of Grótta** *(closed during nesting periods)*. On this little stretch of land, frequented by those seeking beautiful sunsets, you'll find a pretty 19C lighthouse.

On the southern coastline of the commune, around a very windy golf course, are a succession of beaches and creeks. They are often visited by **seals,** who gave their name to the locality. Cross these beaches to walk among the varied residential architecture and enjoy fine views over Bessastaðir (🕯 *p. 40*), the peninsula of Reykjanes and the white cone of Snæfell. As the route goes on, walkers will reach the aerodrome and then Perlan.

ISLAND OFVIÐEY★

B1 *Links by ferry from Skarfabakki harbour located opposite the island, from mid-May to end of Sep.: every hour (outbound: 10.15am-5.15pm, inbound: 11.30am-6.30pm); rest of the year: 3 boats/day.*

36

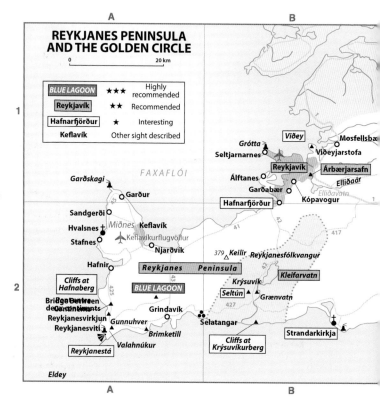

REYKJANES PENINSULA AND THE GOLDEN CIRCLE

0 ————— 20 km

BLUE LAGOON	★★★	Highly recommended
Reykjavík	★★	Recommended
Hafnarfjörður	★	Interesting
Keflavík		Other sight described

FAXAFLÓI

Grótta
Seltjarnarnes
Viðey
Mosfellsbæ
Viðeyjarstofa
Reykjavík
Árbæjarsafn
Elliðaár
Álftanes
Garðabær
Elliðavatn
Hafnarfjörður
Kópavogur

Garðskagi
Garður

Sandgerði
Hvalsnes
Miðnes
Keflavík
Stafnes
Keflavíkurflugvöllur
Njarðvík

379 △ Keilir
Reykjanesfólkvangur
Hafnir

Cliffs at Hafnaberg
Reykjanes Peninsula
Kleifarvatn
Bridge Between the Continents
BLUE LAGOON
Krýsuvík
Reykjanesvirkjun
Seltún
Grænvatn
Grindavík
Reykjanesviti
Gunnuhver
Selatangar
Strandarkirkja
Brimketill
Reykjanestá
Valahnúkur
Cliffs at Krýsuvíkurberg

Eldey

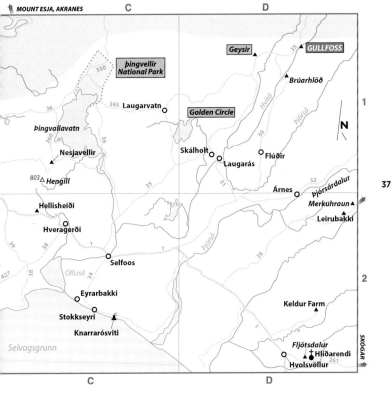

MOUNT ESJA, AKRANES

C

D

Geysir

GULLFOSS

550

Þingvellir
National Park

Brúarhlöð

Hvítá

Þjórsá

365 Laugarvatn

Golden Circle

36

Þingvallavatn

360

36

Skálholt

Laugarás

Flúðir

30

Nesjavellir

N

1

803△ Hengill

35

31

Árnes

Þjórsárdalur

32

37

Merkúhraun

Hellisheiði

Leirubakki

Hveragerði

Þjórsá

39

38

1

1

26

427

38

34

Selfoos

Ölfusá

2

Eyrarbakki

Keldur Farm

Stokkseyri

Knarrarósviti

Selvogsgrunn

1

SKÓGAR

Fljótsdalur

Hlíðarendi

261

Hvolsvöllur

C

D

Viðey Island viewed from Skarfabakki harbour, Mount Esja in the background

© Danuta Hyniewska/age fotostock

Weekends - 1550 kr; connections in summer from the old port to the town center (3/day) and Harpa (2/day) - 🛈 ☏ *533 5055 - http://borgarsogusafn.is/en/videy-island.* Located a stone's throw from the coast, this little chunk of dented earth measuring 1.6 km$^{2/0.6mi}$ provides the opportunity for a few hours of escape from the city. Inhabited since the 10C, the 'wooded isle' (which today has no trees!) would in 1225 see the installation of Augustin monks who would quickly prosper by controlling the surrounding lands. An important medieval **center of culture**, their monastery, which became a last bastion of Catholicism, was destroyed in 1539 during the Reform. At the start of the 20C, a fishery would be installed here doubled by a hamlet, **Sundbakki**. The project would fail however and the last inhabitant left the isle in 1943.

Farther down, the little ferry goes to **Viðeyjarstofa**, the oldest stone farm and oldest original edifice in the country. It was constructed in 1755 for **Skúli Magnússon**, the first Icelandic bailiff. Beautifully renovated (see the cellar), it houses a restaurant *(11am-6pm)*. An adorable pocket-sized church (1774) and the foundations of the former cloister surround it. The rest of the isle offers a veritable playground for ramblers with a selection of cliffs, pebble beaches, basalt columns, ponds and headlands to discover. The omnipresent **birds**, will accompany you everywhere with their alarm calls. Just to the south of the farm, near a small campsite, is the base of the **Imagine Peace Tower**, a column of light designed by Yoko Ono in 2007; it lights up the sky of the capital from October 9 to December 8 (the dates of the birth and death of John Lennon). In the north of the island, visitors may wander among the **ruins** of the hamlet of Sundbakki. By the foundations of each house is displayed the name and role of the family that occupied it.

🚴 The bike routes of the island of Viðey make an exploratory ride easy (bike rental at the old port of Reykjavik free transport on the ferry).

TO THE EAST OF REYKJAVIK

OPEN-AIR MUSEUM OF D'ÁRBÆR★★

(Árbæjarsafn)
B1 À 6 km/3.8mi to the east of the town center - access: bus 19 - Kistuhyl - ✆ 411 6300 - http:// borgarsogusafn.is - June-August: 10am-5pm; rest of the year: 1pm-5pm; guided tours at 1pm, w/o reservation - 1650 kr. Most of the buildings presented here, dating from the 19C and early 20C, have since 1957 come from the capital. They are assembled around Árbær farm, which was founded in the 15C and active until 1948. A journey back through time

and traditions, from the fishermen's house to the farm, the church to the garage.

MOSFELLSBÆR

C1 15 km/9.3mi from the town center. The "moss mountain" is a satellite city in the midst of expansion.
Laxness museum (Gljúfrasteinn) – *Access: bus 18 to Háholt, then bus 27 - ✆ 586 8066 - www.gljufrasteinn. is - June-Aug: daily 9am-5pm; Sep.- May: 10am-4pm except Mon - 900 kr.* On the road from Þingvellir is the fine bourgeois house where **Halldór Laxness** lived. This museum allows readers of this author, who won the **Nobel Prize** for literature in 1955, to get an idea of his daily life

39

Open-Air Museum of D'Arbær

© Markpittimages/Istockphoto.com

and his passions (including collecting art and furniture).

TO THE SOUTH OF REYKJAVIK

B1 Stretching south from Reykjavik, around the bays, peninsulas and hills, these well-appointed communes (replete with parks and cycle routes) offer some curiosities of their own.

KÓPAVOGUR

Access: buses 1, 2 to Hamraborg. Around the little church-shell perches a pretty complex of stone, glass and wood containing a concert room and two museums.
Natural History Museum (Náttúrufræðistofa Kópavogs) – *Hamraborg 6a - ☎ 441 7200 - www.natkop.is - Mon-Thu 9am-6pm, Fri-Sat 11am-5pm - free.* It houses notably "marimos" (moss balls) and a beautiful orca skeleton.
Art Museum (Listasafn Kópavogs-Gerðarsafn) – *Hamraborg 4 - ☎ 570 0440 - www.gerdarsafn.is - daily expt Mon 11am-5pm - 500 kr, free Wed.* On exhibit here are the works of **Gerður Helgadóttir** (stained glasses, sculptures),as well as some contemporary art.

GARÐABÆR

Neighbour of Kópavogur, this residential town is characterized by its coastal roads lined with smart villas.
Museum of Design and Applied Art (Hönnunarsafn Íslands) – *Access: bus 1, then 23 - Garðatorg 1 - ☎ 512 1525 - www.honnunarsafn.is - daily*

except Mon 12pm-5pm - 1000 kr. Situated inland, this museum speaks to the recent push to present and promote Icelandic designers, from 1900 to the present.

ÁLFTANES

Access: bus 1, then 23. Isolated at the end of its flat 'swan peninsula', this villagey area is a solid example of excellent town planning. Here you can make out the white walls and red roofs of the house and chapel (1823) of **Bessastaðir**. The king of Norway established himself in this spot in 1241 in a prairie between the lake and the sea. Seven hundred years later, when Iceland gained its independence, this came to be the site of the president's residence. Isolated and yet in the heart of the agglomeration, the panoramic view from up here is enough to make any visitor consider running as a presidential candidate!

HAFNARFJÖRÐUR★

B1 Access : bus 1, stop: Fjörður - journey 20mn - ℹ *Strandgata 6 - ☎ 585 5500 - www.visithafnarfjordur.is - Mon-Fri 8am-4pm - other office in the museum, June-Aug: 11am-5pm; Sep-May: weekends 11am-5pm.*
Some (not so) old photographs of the **third city of the country** show a creek surrounded by modest houses whose roofs are only just higher than the lava field. The bay remains, as do the houses and the little lava hills in their gardens—transformed into play areas for children—but the waterfront had been modernised and verticalized. The little port, enriched by German

and then English merchants between 14C and 16C, is a pleasant spot to visit. Its museums and maritime space, where you'll find large ships and little dinghies like Optimist offer reason enough to visit.

STRANDGATA

The commercial center **Fjörður** (on the seafront) and Strandgata, the main road, are where you'll find key facilities. From here, small roads such as Austurgata, lined by pretty houses covered in colored steel, can be found nearby. Though they are now separated from the road by new buildings, these quiet streets, as well as some to the north of the bay (Vesturbraut, Kirkjuvegur) are great to wander.

Hafnarborg – *Strandgata 34 - ℘ 585 5790 - http://hafnarborg.is -daily expt Tue 12pm-5pm - free.* Cultural center dedicated to Icelandic artists, from pioneers to contemporary names.

HELLISGERÐI PARK

The black rock at this small park is made up of 7,300-year-old fixed lava and covered in moss interspersed. The site is the crossroads of various "energy lines", meaning it is inhabited by *huldufólk*, the **hidden people** (elves, goblins and other supernatural beings). The tourist office sells a map to help you discover the park and its little grottos and gardens. A guided walk called *Hidden World Walks*, is also on offer (*℘ 694 2785 - www. alfar.is - duration 1hr30min - Jun-Aug: Tue and Fri at 2.30pm; on reservation rest of the year - 4500 kr*).

MUSEUM OF HAFNARFJÖRDUR

Vesturgata 8 - ℘ 585 5780 - www. visithafnarfjordur.is - free.
The city goes to great lengths to educate about its past. The museum is laid out over a number of listed buildings. In **Pakkhúsið** *(Vesturgata 6 - June-Aug: 11am-5pm; Sep.-May: weekends 11am-5pm)*, see the historical exhibition and the one dedicated to old toys. In neighboring, **Síverstens Húsið★** *(June-Aug: 11am-5pm)*, the oldest house in the town (1805), discover the opulent interior of the residence of a rich merchant (mahogany furniture, fine tableware etc.). In the pretty courtyard behind the house, the little Beggubúd boutique *(Vesturgata 6)* houses temporary exhibitions. A short stretch of coast leads to **Siggubær** *(Kirkjuvegur 10 - June-Aug: weekends. 11am-5pm)*, a little fisherman's house inhabited between 1902 and 1978.
⊙ Those interested in the history of maritime trade can pay a visit to **Bookless Bungalow** *(Vesturgata 32 - June-Aug: 11am-5pm)*, constructed by two Scottish brothers who presided over the local fishing industry in the 1920s. The foreign companies that installed themselves in Hafnarfjörður at the start of the 20C are presented here.

Reykjanes Peninsula★★

Because it houses the international airport, the peninsula is often a visitor's first meeting with Iceland—and it makes quite an impression. Divided by the rift between North American and European plates, Reykjanes is a vast lava flow desert, punctuated here and there by carpets of silver moss, vibrant clusters of purple lupin and clouds of smoke, reminding visitors of the intense geothermal activity taking place below. Inhabitants of the area live on the scarce slivers of earth around the big fishing ports, Keflavík to the north and, isolated to the south, Grindavík. Tourists often skip past this little area that has a bit of everything Iceland has to offer geographically: a fissured peninsula, with cliffs sculpted by the lashing ocean and an abundance of bird life. Visitors' heads are (rightfully) turned by one highly colorful attraction—the Blue Lagoon; the sight of it will undoubtedly be one of the highlights of your trip.

▶**Access:** The peninsula of Reykjanes stretches 45km/28mi to the south-west of Reykjavik. The route taking in Reykjavik-Blue Lagoon-Keflavík is well served by public transport, but a car is needed to cross the rest of the peninsula. Leave Reykjavik via Hafnarfjörður (**&** p. 40) and Route 41; it's also possible to follow Route 420 to Vogar, before coming back to Route 41.
Map p. 36-37. Detachable map.
▶**Tips:** If you want to visit the whole of the peninsula, allow a whole day or even a day and a half. You may want to spend a night at Keflavík, Vogar, Grindavík or at the Blue Lagoon. To experience the Blue Lagoon without the crowds, go early in the evening or in the middle of winter.
🛈 Information points at the Grindavík museum (**&** p. 50), the Blue Lagoon (**&** p. 49) and the airport (**&** p. 3).

The **circuit around the perimeter of the peninsula** of Reykjanes stretches for 185km/115mi. Leaving from Reykjavik, you won't need to go far to start to get an idea of the extraordinary geography of this country. The route crosses an immense and dramatic **lava field**, covered by silver moss and framed in the distance by conical hills. The isolated **Keilir** (379m/1243ft) is one of the highest *(B2)*. A shaky route

branches off from Route 41, leading to the desolate flanks.
🐾 Hiking to the top *(return journey from car park 5/6hr for active types)* is not particularly difficult and offers a fine view.

◑ *Leave Route 43 on the left leading to the Lagoon Blue (**&** p. 49) and continue to Njarðvík, entry way to the agglomeration of Reykjanesbær.*

NJARÐVÍK AND KEFLAVÍK
(Reykjanesbær)

A2 *45km/28mi to the south-west of Reykjavík.*
Agglomération of Reykjanesbær: 15,000 inhabitants.

Important trading posts during the Middle Ages, these twin towns are the most important of the agglomeration of **Reykjanesbær**. Visitors coming from or going to the international airport will pass through them quickly (the large areas of low, wind-resistant houses are not particularly captivating). However, the area is a good starting point for exploring the region.

From 1949 to 2006, American soldiers and their families occupied a vast base to the south of the city, living in a collection of buildings with pink, green and cream roofs, which the local population are slowly making their own. The area is still marked by the presence of the **US Army**, which for fifty years provided a living for one-fifth of the region's working population. Along **Njarðarbraut** and **Hafnargata**, which constitute the main area of the district, you'll find a succession of shops, car parks, drive-ins and fast-food joints, reminiscent of an American small town; you'll even find some cafés that wouldn't look out of place on the set of a remake of *Happy Days*.

NJARÐVÍK

To the south-east of Keflavík, Njarðvík creates an attraction of its Viking past.

Víkingaheimar – *Víkingabraut 1 -* ✆ *422 2000 - www.vikingaheimar.is - Feb-Oct 7am-6pm, Nov-Jan: 10am-5pm - 1500 kr.* ♟♟ In the crook of the bay, the modern **Viking Wave** building houses a museum dedicated to Vikings and more specifically to their maritime expeditions. The star is the reconstitution of *Gokstad*, a Viking boat discovered in Norway in the 19C. Renamed *Íslendingur*, this copy crossed the Atlantic to New York in 2000 to commemorate **Leif Eriksson's** discovery of the United States. The evocation of Nordic mythology and the archaeological discoveries of the region complete the exhibition.

Outside, not far from a small petting zoo, you'll find **Stekkjarkot** *(booking,* ✆ *420 3240)*, a little farm with a grass roof that was inhabited between 1855 and 1924.

▶ *Head in the direction of Keflavík Center (Keflavík Miðbær).*

KEFLAVÍK

After heading up the very Americanized Njarðabraut, you';l need to drive to the end of Hafnargata to come back to Iceland. There, along Túngata or Vallargata, between the town hall and so-called "small boats" port *(Gróf)*, you'll find a line of houses in wood and colorful corrugated steel. On the nearby sea front is a vast stretch of grass (sometimes the site of festivals), which is decorated with an imposing sculpture of **Àsmundur Sveinsson**. The historic heritage here is modest but well demonstrated around the little **Gróf port**.

Duushús★ – *Duusgata 2-8 - ℘ 420 3245 - 12h-17h - 1500 kr.* **≗** Cultural center of Keflavík, the **museum** in installed in a set of beautiful listed buildings. Dating from 1877, the port house was at the time the second biggest building in the country after the Parliament. It was constructed for the rich Danish merchant Hans Peter Duus to serve as a workers' warehouse. The neighboring houses were used for treating and conserving fish. During the visit, you'll discover an impressive armada of **model boats★★** from the 19C and start of the 20C, built by Grímur Karlsson, a modeling enthusiast. The other rooms are used for temporary artistic and folkloric exhibitions. Chosen themes put the emphasis on the **history and daily life of the region** and its inhabitants (examples include exhibits dedicated to one locality, the 1970s, living by a NATO base, etc.). The neighboring café is a great spot to take a break and contemplate the sea.

≗ On the other side of the port, a **giant** snores in an artificial grotto *(10am-5pm)*. The enormous sculpture of this character created in 1959 by children's book author **Herdís Egilsdóttir** was made by a collective of artists for the Winter Lights Festival in 2008.

▶ *Leave the little port of Keflavík in the direction of Garður via Route 45.*

Shared tracks

Every year more and more planes hit the runway at Keflavík International Airport (Keflavíkurflugvöllur). Construction began in May 1942 under the name Meek Fields, initiated by the US Army in the middle of the Second World War, and was used as an air supply base. When the conflict ended, civil airplanes came to use the same route, but then in 1952, the Americans reestablished themselves here under the NATO flag. From this time, the airport was managed jointly by Icelanders and the military, a source of controversy and debate for many decades. This is understandable when we imagine that until 1987, travelers were obliged to pass through military checkpoints because the commercial terminal was located within the military periphery. In the same year, the commercial terminal, named Leif Eiríksson, was established. Air traffic was still co-managed until 2006, when the US troops left.

With its two 3,000m-long runways, the airport can accommodate the largest of planes, and even a spaceship. Airlines around the world use these runways as training grounds to get their pilots used to landing in strong winds and snow. The enormous present-day terminal, which was expanded between 2001 and 2007, is known for its comfort. Two contemporary sculptures embellish the approach to the airport: "Regnbogi" (Rainbow) by Rúrí, with its colored glass mosaic that sparkles in the sun, and "Þotuhreiður" (Jet nest) by Magnús Tómasson, which seems to represent the birth of a Concorde from an egg!

THE WEST COAST – FROM KEFLAVÍK TO GRINDAVÍK★

The west coast, followed by the tranquil Routes 45 and 425, is embellished with little villages, humid zones and lava fields that run towards the sea and are met by either beach or cliffs.

GARÐUR AND GARÐSKAGI

A1 9km from Keflavík.1,450 inhab.
As you cross the village of Garður, you'll see a **chapel** from 1863, before continuing on to the Garðskagi cape. At the end of the strip of **Miðnes**, two **lighthouses** (from1897 and 1944) guard a little cape frequented by flocks of sea birds. This is one of the countless end-of-the-world locations that characterize Iceland. The wind blows heartily here, sometimes too strongly for the few campers' tents you'll find dotted about at any given time. Visitors come here for the view over Snæfellsnes peninsula (when the weather is clear), which stretches to the north, and to take in the magnificent sunset; in winter this is a site for spotting the Aurora Borealis.

Garðskagi Museum – *Skagabraut 100 - 𝒫 422 7220 - www.sagatrail.is - 1pm-5pm - restaurant - 400 kr.* Located near Iceland's tallest lighthouse (28m/92ft) is this museum with its impressive collection of bric-a-brought together by an enthusiastic collector. You'll find motors, everyday objects, agricultural machines, skiffs, phone directories and birds' eggs! An interesting

cross-section of local life.
Get back on to Route 45, in the direction of Sandgerði.

SANDGERÐI

A2 7 km/4mi from Garður. 1,700 inhab.
This fishing village, whose name means "sand barrier" is one of the most populated of the region. It's built on a sandy coast, and the humid zone that surrounds it is covered in nesting season by thousands of birds. On your way in to the village, in the port area, you'll find the Nature Center.

≗≗ Sandgerði Nature Center (Þekkingarsetur Suðurnesja) – *Garðvegi 1 - 𝒫 423 7551 - http://thekkingarsetur.is - May-Sep: 10am-4pm, weekends 1pm-5pm; Oct-Apr: Mon-Fri 10am-2pm - 600 kr.* The stuffed local fauna is not presented with great flair, but visitors will appreciate the many birds and a fine walrus (the animal also figures on the shield of the village). Aquariums complete the exhibit.

◖ *Cross the village in the direction of, direction Stafnes.*

At the exit for Sandgerði, from June to August, the narrow road cuts through **the air territory of terns**, geese and ducks, ensuring you an aerial flyover en route. It passes **Hvalsnes (A2)** raising its small tricolored steeple since 1887. **Stafnes (A2)** is where you'll find a little stone and basalt church with a clock tower. In the following hamlet, an important winter fishing station, is a dominating yellow lighthouse used between

© Lee Frost/age fotostock

47

Aurora Borealis, Garður

16C and 18C. It's hard to imagine that its neighbors, **Básendar** (destroyed in 1799 by a tidal wave) and **Þórshöfn** were once major commercial sites.

❯ *At the junction with Route 425, head in the direction of Hafnir, to the right.*

THE SOUTHWEST POINT★

A2 Seemingly occupied since the first decades of colonization by the brother of Ingólfur Arnarson, who claimed possession of the whole region, **Hafnir** is today a minuscule hamlet of fisherpeople dotted around its little black church. As you leave the village the landscape changes

dramatically. The strip of asphalt winds a route through an **immense lava flow**, in the area of one hundred craters. As in the rest of the peninsula, these lava fields are relatively young (around the 13C.).

🐾 A discreet car park can be found at the start of a route leading to the **Hafnaberg Sea-cliffs★**. After 30min of walking from cairn to cairn amid a lunar landscape, you'll reach the coastline, which is known among ornithologists for its guillemot population.

Next, the road will lead to the **Bridge between two continents** (Brú milli heimsálfa), a bridge spanning a fault line between European and North

American plates, a symbolic site and a great place for a photo.

You'll find another car park a little farther on, close to a small crater where a 5min climb allows views of the surrounding area—a strikingly desolate spot that is even more impressive under heavy grey clouds. The landscape is black and scorched; on the horizon you'll see plumes of smoke from across the ocean and the little island of Eldey.

The sudden apparition of the metal hangars of **Reykjanesvirkjun**, the geothermal power station of Reykjanes, is a pleasing surprise. **Power Plant Earth** (Orkuverið Jörð) – ☏ 436 1000 - May-Sep 12.30pm-4.30pm - www.facebook.com/powerplantearth - 1500 kr. is a very well done interactive exhibition presented on the site of the power station is centerd round energy sources.

Visitors can also appreciate the wild and desolate landscape around the hill of **Valahnúkur**, at the south-west tip of the peninsula, criss-crossed by paths. Here you'll find **Reykjanesviti** lighthouse, constructed on the headland of Bæjarfell (73m/240ft) in 1907 to replace a 1887 incarnation—then the first in the country—destroyed by an earthquake.

From here, there's a **beautiful view**★★ over the cliffs of **Reykjanestá**★ to the south and the smoke of the **Gunnuhver** thermal zone to the east. With a circumference of 20m/65ft, its crater of boiling mud is the largest in the country. **Eldey** rises up in the distance, the 'island of fire, which will spurt during an underwater eruption.

Black and striped by the basalt columns of its 77m/253ft cliffs, it brings to mind finely made layer cake fresh out the mold. A reserve farmed to the public, the isle is invaded every year by 70,000 Bassan enthusiasts (www.eldey.is). The fish-filled but highly dangerous surrounding waters were frequented by French schooners at the turn of the 19C and 20C.

Route 425 forks out to the west. A path signposted on the right leads quickly to **Brimketill**, a curious formation of lava in the shape of a giant cauldron, which puts up a brave fight against the lashings of the ocean.

BLUE LAGOON★★★

(Bláa Lónið)

A2 50km/31mi to the south-west of Reykjavik – ☏ 420 8800 - www.bluelagoon.com - ⚬ - Jun: 7am-11pm, Jul-Aug: 7am-12am, Sep: 8am-10pm, Oct-Dec: 8am-9pm, rest of the year: 8am-10pm -from 6990 kr - ATM, baggage lockers, restaurant, café and souvenir shop.

☺ **Important** : the popularity of the Lagoon is such that you now need to reserve in advance online. Iceland's number one attraction is characterized by columns of **white smoke** that surge abruptly from moss-covered **lava**. It's a geothermal factory complete with chimneys and silver pipes and, of course, that **improbably blue** water which mingles with the black volcanic rock in jets. It was in 1976 that it was decided to spread the surplus water of the geothermal factory of Svartsengi

between the rocks and the lava. In 1981, Icelanders started to come and bathe here, and in 1987, the first infrastructure was created. Though equipped only with modest changing rooms at the start, its naming was a stroke of marketing ingenuity and the Blue Lagoon grew until it became an attraction known the world over. Today, bathing without many others nearby is challenging. Once you've crossed the (ever-growing) car park and bought your (rather expensive) ticket, you may then—depending on the season—be sharp-elbowed to get a good spot. But, despite the discouraging entrance procedure, the magic of the site itself never falters. In winter or quieter hours (the evening), you do have a real chance of enjoying a bit of isolation.

The phenomenal success of the attraction is due to the entirely unique experience of bathing there. The water is up to 1,800 m/5905ft deep and slightly salty, with the temperature reaching heights of 240°C. Rich in seaweed, silica, limestone and sulphate (hence the smell), the milky blue turquoise of the lake is singularly striking. This combined with the sometimes-smoke-spitting pipes and the jet black lava that surrounds the site, create an ambiance worthy of a science-fiction film. Once you have thoroughly washed and removed all jewelery, lower yourself into the **38°C** water by way of soft wooden decking. The mud that carpets the bottom of the basin and with which bathers cover themselves is luxuriously soft. The temperature varies; in the places where the water comes out, the degrees climb significantly. "Hot pots", a waterfall, a sauna and a hammam await at the west of the basin.

🐌 The color and temperature of the water varies depending on the weather (sun, wind, rain, snow) and under the stars at nightfall, changing in turn the different sensations on offer. It's a must to take a dip **after landing** or just before your **return flight**. On-site you'll also find Lava restaurant, massage facilities, private lounges and a raised platform view, offering the best spot for **photos**. Only this last option is free.

GRINDAVÍK

A2 🅱 *www.visitgrindavik.is*
2840 inhab. The only locality in the south of Reykjanes, Grindavík is one of the country's most important **fishing ports**. In the Middle Ages, the merchants of the Hanse and from England traded—and at times came to blows—in this little village, of which the activity would also attract pirates from Algeria. They raged during their looting expedition to the south coast in June 1627.

The docks, which house shipping companies and warehouses, account for a large part of the village. At boat level, you'll find a constant ballet of moving forklifts and crates of fish stacked on top of each other like a giant Tetris game; through the sometimes-open gates you may catch glimpses of the industrial treating and freezing processes.

Saltfish Museum★ (Saltfisksetur Íslands) – *Inside the Kvikan complex, Hafnargata 12a - ℘ 420 1190 - www.grindavik.is - summer: weekends 10am-5pm, winter: w/e 11am-5pm - 1200 kr.*

Quite naturally, the main attraction of Grindavík is dedicated to **fishing in Iceland**. The museum contains a small exhibition themed around this activity, which focuses in particular on the salting and drying of the saltfish. It's an interesting and well-laid-out display comprising wax models, short films, photos, objects and a background soundtrack of seagull cries. The exhibit follows the chronological evolution of working conditions (decked boats only replaced small fishing boats at the start of the 20C!), as well as fish conservation and fishing and trading techniques.

Visitors will learn about the economic importance of saltfish **export** to a number of countries—Spain, Portugal, Greece, Brazil—and how dependent this crucial trade is on the machinations of international politics. For example, to win the Spanish market instead of Norway, Icelanders had to agree to import Iberian wine and to soften their alcohol prohibition laws (which Norway would refuse). After the Second World War, freezing would replace drying-salting, and the saltfish, formerly the fish of the poorer population, would become a more luxurious product. The practice of drying would continue, however, thanks to exports to Africa.

Jarðoka, an exhibition comprised of 18 panels, is themed around energy;

it is instructive but a little less interesting.

If you're spending longer in Grindavík, you may or may not appreciate the **port atmosphere**, which some find romantic and others a little depressing! Soak it all in one of the cafés or restaurants around the port.

❍ *Leave Grindavík to the east via Route 427, which has recently been recovered in asphalt.*

THE SOUTH OF REYKJANES★★

BC2 The road begins by winding round a brown-colored hilly formation, which the ocean has lashed into imposing cliffs. It once more crosses a vast, desolate lava field covered in parts with moss. It's hard to imagine that this coastline could have been inhabited. The site of **Selatangar** (*signposted on the right*) was however a winter fishing station, active until 1884. The ruins of lava stone fishermans' huts are still visible. After 22km/13mi, Route 427 passes through the **Reykjanesfólkvangur** nature reserve. A track verges off right towards **Krýsuvíkurberg**★ and a set off cliffs that are favorites among ornithologists. Enthusiasts can follow the road that overhangs them for 4km/2.5mi and observe puffins, guillemots, petrels and perhaps even some seals.

❍ *From Route 427, take Route 42 on the left in the direction of Seltún and Krýsuvík.*

© Promote Iceland

Lake Kleifarvatn

KRÝSUVÍK

B2 25km/15.5mi from Reykjavik.
Located on the main seam of the
rift, this geothermal region takes the
name of a now abandoned church.
First stop: **Grænvatn**, the "green lake"
lodged in an old crater, which takes
its name from the seaweed that gives
it its color.

Seltún★ – Plumes of smoke announce
the multicolored hilly formation of
this geothermal field. Amid a strong
sulphuric odor, follow wooden paths
which slalom between columns
of smoke, boiling mud bogs and
different colored solfataras.
*The next road, unpaved, reaches
another lake after a few kilometers.*
Kleifarvatn Lake★★ – Its name evokes
a fissure, the deep, volcanic one,

which it in part covers. After a seism
in 2000, its water level significantly
diminished. This periodic 'draining'
process inspired author Arnaldur
Indriðason's novel *The Draining
Lake* (2006), which starts with
the discovery of a skeleton in the
suddenly-revealed mud at Kleifarvatn.
☜ Walk the loop of the lake to
photograph the beaches and black
cliffs (and to look out for the aquatic
monster that just may lurk below!)

❍ *You can come back to Reykjavik via
Route 42 or come back on the 427 and
continue east towards Hveragerði and
Selfoss.*

Route 427 continues to the east
passing craggy hills and mountain
through fixed lava covered in wooly

moss *(Racomitrium lanuginosum)*. At some points it forms a thick (and moist) carpet that shimmers a brilliant green or glints of silver depending on the humidity level in the ground. After 24km/15mi, you'll see a clutch of houses.

▶ *Take the right turn and follow the signs saying "Strandarkirkja".*

STRANDARKIRKJA★

C2 60km/37mi from Reykjavik - May-Sep: 9am-7pm.
This sweet little church sits on the edge of the sea, sheltered by a dyke and set apart from **Selvogur**. Equipped with a lighthouse since 1931, this lost hamlet was once more populated, despite its location on a narrow band of not very fertile earth, as well as the difficulty of accessing the sea in its position. The church was constructed in 1888, undoubtedly on the site of an older church, whose foundation reportedly dates back to the 13C; it owes its charm to its remarkable isolation. The interior is a haven of calm with its bright sky-blue interior, star-covered vault, salmon-colored walls, wood floor and carpet, in sharp contrast to the wind howling outside. Each year it welcomes a significant pilgrimage of fisherpeople and sailors.

▶ *Route 427 continues towards Þorlákshöfn, where Route 38,then the 1, lead to Hveragerði, and the 34 towards Selfoss via Eyrarbakki.*

© ARCO/Scholz, F/age fotostock

Strandarkirkja

The Golden Circle★★

Russia has its Ring of Fire, Southeast Asia has its Golden Triangle, and Iceland has its very own Golden Circle. Linking three emblematic sites surrounding the capital, this circuit—on the program for just about every tour company and very busy in summer—enjoys well-deserved success. Þingvellir brings together historical interest and natural beauty; Geysir is a quintessential demonstration of its meaning, "geyser", while Gullfoss, the Golden Waterfall, offers rainbows and a symphony for your eardrums . If you have time to get off the well-beaten track, you can discover the spots where the inhabitants of the capital go to relax—a variety of landscapes taking in old farms, waterfalls and welcoming hot springs. All this in the shadow of the awe-inspiring Hekla volcano.

▶**Access:** You have two routes to choose from as you leave Reykjavik. For the most direct: head north out the capital on Route 1 (towards Akranes) then to Mosfellsbær; turn right at Route 36, in the direction of Þingvellir. Between June and October, choose the scenic option taking Route 435. Head south out of Reykjavik taking Route 1 (towards Selfoss); as you leave the city, turn left on Route 435, in the direction of Nesjavellir.

Map p. 36-37. Detachable map.

▶**Tip:** Despite the cold, it's still well worth adding the Golden Circle to your itinerary in winter, when the precious glimmers of light embellish the scenery and visitors are fewer.

🛈 Information points at **Þingvellir Tourist Information Center** (⏱ *p. 56*) and Geysir Center (⏱ *p 62*).

TOWARDS ÞINGVELLIR ON ROUTE 435★

C1 After a hilly stretch, **Route 435** crosses a plate of the tundra of **Mosfellsheiði**, very close to the shiny pipe that provides the capital's hot water. The horizon opens to reveal a 360° view taking in the surrounding black and red snow-capped hills. After 18km/11mi, the road rises and so will your adrenalin levels as the drive begins to feel a bit like a fairground ride (15° slopes, tight corners) as you scale winding rock formations,

which have provided the backdrop to various car ads. You'll see smoke rising up suddenly from some ridges. Then, at the last hairpin bend, you'll be rewarded wit a beautiful view over **Lake Þingvallavatn**.

Nesjavellir Geothermal Power Station (*www.or.is*). Before taking a tour around the lake, make a brief detour to the smoke-plume-draped valley that houses this power station that spits with the deafening sound of a blower. At the foot of the **Hengill** volcano, the geothermal activity is phenomenal. Drawn from 2km/1.2mi

under the ground, the water, which reaches 360°C, heats the capital and serves the electric power plant in **Hellisheiði** to the south.

Between the south of the lake and Hveragerði, you'll find various walking routes (*good map necessary - 12-14km/7.5mi-8.5mi - all levels*) either going round or tackling the summit (803m/2634ft) of **Hengill volcano**, whose last eruption was around 2,000 years ago.

Þingvellir is reached by **Route 360** which follows the west side of the lake; you'll spot farms and little isolated cottages in a green valley landscape.

◆ *At the crossroads with Route 36, head in the direction of Þingvellir. Þingvellir Tourist Information Center is located nearby on the right.*

ÞINGVELLIR NATIONAL PARK★★

(Þingvellir Þjóðgarður)

C1 50km/31ft to the northeast of Reykjavik.

Þingvellir Information Center – Þjónustumidstöð - ☎ 482 2660 - *www.thingvellir.is - Jun-Aug: 9am-10pm (6pm rest of the year).* This center houses a tourist information point, as well as a café, toilets and a reception for the campsites of the national park (**☞** *"Where to Stay", p. 82*).This is where the buses on regular lines stop.

Protected since 1928 and **UNESCO** listed in 2004, Þingvellir National Park combines natural beauty and historical interest. It is in this spot, on the edge of the country's largest lake

A plan for a parliament

In the year 930 the first Icelanders chose this graben (ditch) as the meeting place where their parliament would be installed. The choice of the site, then called 'Bláskógar' and renamed Þingvellir ('the plain of parliament'), is explained by a number of factors including the majesty of the site, the proximity of a fishing lake and ample firewood, a dramatic cliff fit for speeches and a plain on which to hold debates. The area was also already inhabited and was located at the crossroads of various routes.

Between 930 and 1262, AlÞing ruled over Iceland, legislating, judging, and choosing the religion of the country. Every year the annual assembly of clan heads would also attract merchants, poets and peasants. The two-week meeting offered a unique chance for the sparse and scattered population to meet in order to negotiate, create agreements, settle disputes - and indulge in a spot of revelry. Despite annexation by Norway and then the Danish yoke, Icelanders continued to gather in Þingvellir until 1798, when the AlÞing was transferred to Reykjavik. Having lost none of its stature, it was logically chosen as the site of the 1,000-year anniversary of colonization celebration in 1874, as well as the writing of the Constitution. The poets and writers at the helm of the independence movement would have Þingvellir as a sacred site and a symbol of their cause. On June 17, 1944, it was here that Independence was declared and the republic of Iceland was created. Halldór Laxness wrote in Þingvellir, "every Icelander feels almost physically the thousand-year-old call of their history."

and along parallel fault lines, that the first settlers created the **Alþing**, the original democratic parliament.
As you arrive from Reykjavik, it's difficult to imagine the tundra suddenly collapsing, but Þingvellir is located on the **Mid-Atlantic Ridge** which crosses Iceland, the seat of some significant tectonic activity: it's a rift marking the movement of the Earth's crust, torn between the Eurasian and North American plates, which are drifting 5mm/.20in per year. This phenomenon is manifested most spectacularly by the series of beautiful long, wide parallel cracks that streak the landscape. They point towards **Lake Þingvallavatn** (83km^2/ 32 mi^2 and 115m/377ft deep), fed by Langjökull glacier, located 70km/20ft to the north. Dotted with second homes where the inhabitants of Reykjavik come to spend the summer, the banks are decorated by lava flows covered with moss and clutches of willows and dwarf birches which blaze with color in autumn. The lake waters, populated by Arctic char and stickleback, attract fishing fishers, as well as various species of birds (swans, tourniquets, scaup, mergansers, geese, birds of prey and more). In recent years, Silfra's submerged fault line (and the site of Davíðsgká) increasingly draws pro divers, who explore its blue-tinted water, considered the clearest in the world. With a constant temperature of 4°C, it offers visibility up to 100m/328ft.

VISITOR CENTER

☏ 482 3613 - www.thingvellir.is - June-Aug: 9am-7pm; rest of the year : 9am-6.30pm - free.
From the platform of the center, called **hakið**, the view offers all the elements of the site's geology: the lake and its islands, the faults and the smoke at the foot of Hengill. You'll find comprehensive explanations of the panorama on touch screens inside the building. Be sure to grab a map of the national park before exploring. There are free ranger-guided tours twice a day (10am and 2pm); meeting point in front of the church.

SITE OF THE ALÞING

If you would prefer not to walk, you can reach the site and its various points of interest by car (by Route 361).
Almannagjá – or "gorge of the Ancients" is the largest fissure in the region. The beautiful river Öxará cascades here via the waterfall of **Öxarárfoss★** and boils between the black rocks.
A wide path descends along the cliffs towards the plain, through the many fault lines; along the way, you'll see waterfalls pass into little pools, while little scratch-mark-like cracks are filled with clear water that reflects the clouds above.
This is a place to contemplate the power of nature, and to ponder the area's history, highlighted in its place names: were witches burned in Brennugjá (ardent chasm)? Were allegedly adulterous women thrown

into the Drekkingarhykur (drowning pool)? The **Alþing** convened at the **Lögberg** (Rock of the Law), where the *lögsögumaður* said the law before the assembly. Two sites of the Lögberg can still be visited today: the original, close to the fault line of Flosagjá and that of the Christian era at the foot of the Almannagjá. You will also see some **búðir** ruins, remnants of earth- and grass-covered stone shelters , which housed the participants at the Alþing. They dated from the 17C and 18C.

Guided by helpful information panels, you'll be led to the foot of the cliffs by a pair of buildings whose white walls stand out in the black-green-blue landscape.

Þingvallabær – A photogenic sight with its saw-tooth roof, this farm was built in 1930 on the 1,000-year anniversary of Alþing and now serves as a summer residence for the Prime Minister and as the National Park's head office.

Þingvallakirkja – *from mid-May to early Sep: 9am-5pm.* The church of the *Bello of Iceland* of Halldór Laxness dates from 1859, but stands on the site of one of the country's first churches. Inside, various elements come from earlier churches: bells, a painted altarpiece (1834) and pulpit (17C). Within, poets Jónas Hallgrímsson and Einar Benediktsson, bards of the independence movement, lay at rest. Nearby, you'll find the **Biskupabúð**, the oldest *búðir* of Þingvellir, which housed the bishops of Iceland during special meetings.

ÞINGVALLAHRAUN AND THE LAKESIDE

🔊 Beyond extends a lava field, spat out by the **Skjaldbreiður** shield volcano (which stands 50km/19mi to the north). You'll see a great expanse of black rock embellished with ripples of moss, dispersing into the lake in the shape of a number of photogenic islands. Walkers criss- cross this area via various paths that converge on the abandoned farms of Skógarkot (inhabited until 1936) and Þórhallastaðir (a brewery farm from the 13C).

▷ *Those traveling in cars will come back on Route 36.*

Just after exiting the Visitor Center car park, the road passes the Öxará river before the flow is swallowed suddenly by a fault line. You can park here and in a few short paces be looking **Öxarárfoss waterfall★** (📖 *p. 57*).

▷ *Route 36 passes in front of Þingvellir Information Center. Here, you can head in the direction of Laugarvatn/Geysir by continuing on Route 36 or take the 361 (which rejoins the 36 a little farther on, to the east of the lake).*

Route 361 goes along the fault line, before coming back around Þingvallabær, all the while taking in fine views of the lake. Þingvellir soon stretches into the distance in the rear view mirror, a great scar overhanging the lake. Cast one more look at the snow-capped peaks before discovering Lake Laugarvatn, with its

© Denis Caviglia/hemis.fr

Öxarárfoss waterfall

stunning yet frightening silhouette of the Hekla, the "door of Hell", rising up above.

LAUGARVATN

C1 25km/15.5mi to the east of Þingvellir. 250 inhab.
The **hot spring lake** attraction is comprised of both the lake itself and the minuscule locality that flanks its west side. Its name is indicative of the reasons Icelanders come here: for calm, quiet and bathing. Aside from a few large school buildings, the village is limited to a few dwellings, mostly secluded second homes, nestled among the conifers and miniature birches that line the lake.

If you're crossing the Golden Circle without a tour company, Laugarvatn is an ideal place to take a break, stock up on supplies (gas, food) or spend the night. Be sure to pay a visit to the **Reykhúsið Útey fish smoke house** (*Útey 1 - Bláskógabyggð - ℘ 486 1194 - www.utey.is - summer: 9am-7pm*), located to the south of the lake (Route 364); locals come here for the fine trout, salmon and Arctic char.

VÍGÐULAUG

The plumes of steam that rise from this **hot spring**, which are even thicker in rainy weather, attracted settlers to the lake's banks in the Middle Ages. After the adoption of Christianity, baptisms were practiced here. The basin that sits below the excellent restaurant Lindin (👁 *"Where to Eat", p. 68*) is evocative of the long legacy of bathing in this hot spring. Legend states that this is where the body of **Jón Arason**, the country's last Catholic bishop, was bathed; he was executed with his sons in 1550 in Skálholt. This rural town around 25km /15mi to the south-east, was from 1056 to 1797, the seat of the diocese of the South of Iceland.

Laugarvatn Fontana – *Hverabraut 1 - 🖉 486 1400 - www.fontana.is; Aug: 10am-11pm - rest of the year: 11am-10pm - 3800 kr.* These thermal baths are not quite in the same league as the Blue Lagoon. The basins (water at 40-50 °C) are arranged in a curious design with a long, narrow layout meaning it is impossible to find an isolated spot. The pluses : sublime wintry light, as well as a sauna and hammam on the edge of the lake. You may also wish to take a dip in the pool or appreciate the calm waters of the lake in a small row boat or kayak *(if you don't find anyone at the pier, try the campsite reception or hostel)*. If you want to add a splash of adventure, try your hand at caving in the lava tunnels (👁 *"Caving", p. 106*).

Laugarvatnsfjall mountain – 🥾 *1hr - all levels. Leave Laugarvatn by Route37 (dir. Geysir).* The road winds through a verdant landscape between modest peaks and the plain (re)planted here and there with groves. **Route 37** becomes **35** and the plumes of steam that

rise between hills on the horizon announce Geysir.

GEYSIR ★★

D1 *25km/15.5mi to the east of Laugarvatn.*
In the valley of **Haukadalur**, a high seat of culture during the Middle Ages, Geysir is easily the most frequented geothermal zone in the country. Across more than 3km^2 /1.15mi^2, at the foot of the rhyolitic hill of Laugarfjall, you'll find a rather impressive panoply: hot water springs; multi-colored crystals; plumes of smoke escaping from the fissures whistling like a casserole dishes; bubbling grey and beige mud puddles—but also a discreet spread of vegetation around the hot springs. These often go unnoticed by the ever-increasing flocks of visitors as they head straight to the main attraction, the **geysers** (👁 *p. 62*). The Icelandic verb *gjosa* (to gush out) gives its name to this spectacular phenomenon, which only a few countries in the world (New Zealand, the US and Japan) can advertise in their tourist brochures.

GEYSIR CENTER

Geysisstofa - 🖉 480 6800 - www. geysircenter.com - 9am-7pm.
Geysir has become a sort of amusement park, which from May to September attracts a huge number of tourists. You will rarely have the opportunity to be alone at Strokkur as you capture *the* moment on your camera. The Geysir Center, which grows a little in size every year,

houses a multimedia exhibition dedicated to geothermal phenomena *(summer: 10am-5pm; rest of the year: 12pm-4pm - 1000 kr)*, as well as a café-food shop, a little restaurant *(10am-5pm)*, a huge gift shop and the welcome desk for the neighboring campsite.

THE GEYSERS

The Great Geysir – 👤👤

Of the two star geysers, the Great Geysir is undoubtedly the most impressive. It has been shooting again since 2000, after several decades of enforced hibernation; it projects a column of water 15-25m (49-82ft) high, unfortunately at a rather irregular rate (every 2-3 days). It is certainly impressive, but a little

© Ocs_12/iStockphoto.com

Golden plover

Golden plover means springtime

The photogenic puffin that populates the coastal cliffs may be the star of postcards and souvenir shops, but another less glamorous bird still occupies a special place in the heart of Icelanders. Each year, they eagerly await the return of the golden plover, which announces much-awaited spring. With its black belly and speckled brown head, wings and back, this fine migrating bird blends into the background of the lava fields it moves through. A white 'S' stretches across its body from eye to tail, a little design touch that is recreated with affection by watercolor painters and sculptors. Tucked away in mosses occurring in altitudes below 500m/1,640ft, you'll encounter these birds as soon as you go off the main roads. You can detect them by their melancholic little cry, a brief call, thrown out from the bird's branch perch. During laying season (May-June) perhaps you'll witness the well-practiced show of the female who, to discourage you from approaching her nest, will feign injury. In October, when the plover flies off to Eastern Europe, Icelanders know that the good weather is well and truly over for the year. They immediately restart the clock waiting for the migrating bird that is always the first to return to the island of volcanoes.

The very exclusive club of countries with geysers

Depending as it does upon very specific geological and climate particularities, the phenomenon of a geyser exists only in a handful of countries, as well as some underwater zones. Yellowstone National Park (Wyoming, US) is home to two thirds of the world's geysers; among them is 'Old Faithful', a fountain type geyser that ejects a 40m/131ft spray of water and steam every 75mins, and 'Steamboat', which holds the current world record for the highest jet, at 110m/360ft. This is a small fry compared to the 400m/1,312ft column of muddy water briefly spat out (1899-1904) by an almighty explosion of Waimangu ('black water') in New Zealand.

Other parts of the world with intense volcanic activity are home to various geysers on different scales. The Russian peninsula of Kamtchatk still has memories of its valley of geysers, unfortunately damaged by an earthquake in 2007. There are also some in Japan near Nagano, at the bottom of the Mahawu crater in Sulawesi (Indonesia), on the site of Del Tatio situated at 4,200m /13780ft altitude in Chile (80 small geysers not exceeding 6m/19ft) and in the Azores, Portugal. In Kenya, around Lake Bogoria and in Dallol in Ethiopia, in a salty hollow 120m/394ft below water level, little gassy geysers are busy spurting. Even smaller are those on the island of Saint Lucia, which are barely 50cm/20in high.

sad compared to what it was at the height of its form: from its first historical mention in 1294 all the way up until 1950, it reportedly rose 60-80m (197-262ft) high **.Strokkur – 👤👤**
Neighbour of the Great Geysir, the geysir known as Strokkur ("churn") is not nearly as strong. Mentioned in records since 1789, it does however offer regular shows roughly every 10min gushing out 20-35m/65-115ft torrents of water. The process of reaching crescendo is fascinating. Visitors begin by approaching the geyser vent, a siliceous stone crown in a beautiful grey color. Profound beats, evocative of a great heartbeat, suddenly vibrate the ground, the first hint of the bubbling life underneath. A huge, hypnotizing blue bubble forms before exploding violently and vertically upwards. The jet either blasts straight or is blown off course by the wind, before falling in a fine rain of hot water (see if you can escape its drops!).

👁 There is a hillside walking path that leads to a peak where you can admire the spectacle from above.
Leave Geysir following Route 35 in the direction of Gullfoss.
The landscape will change quickly and soon the ice cap of Langjökull will whitens the horizon, while black peaks announce the Highlands.

GULLFOSS★★★

D1 15km/9mi to the north-east of Geysir. Two car parks: the first gives access to the site from the bottom; the second (and most-visited) from the top, close to the Gullfoss Kaffi.

Falling from Langjökull, the river Hvítá flows into a deep and narrow fissure. Gullfoss, the magnificent **Golden Waterfall**, takes its name from the rainbow that colors it from time to time, forming an iridescent bridge between the two banks; 32m/105ft high, the cascade progresses in stages (11m /36ft, then 21m/69ft), taking in a change of direction, and ends with a fearsome and deafening explosion of moss. The river then continues its course between the basalt organs of 2.5km (1.5mi)-long gorges, which it has been hollowing out for centuries.

From the road, if it weren't for the groups of parked cars, you would pass the foot of one of the country's most beautiful waterfalls without seeing it! Before or after admiring this natural treasure, you can stop in at the **Gullfoss Kaffi** restaurant (☎ 486 6500 - http://gullfoss.is - summer: 9am-9.30pm; rest of the year: 10am-7pm), which is likely to be announced by the aroma of lamb soup (the house specialty). You'll also find a huge gift shop where you can snap up local crafts. The site of the Gullfoss owes much to **Sigríður Tómasdóttir** who, at the start of the 20C, fought to prevent the construction of a hydroelectric power station by the falls at a supercharged output (130m³/s).

CATARACTE ★★★

👥 A wooden path lined with information boards bypasses the Gullfoss Center, leaving the stark landscape to dominate. A staircase descends towards the waterfall and several paths approach it or overhang it. Your senses will be awakened by the changing colors, the rising and descending cadence of the waterfall's roar, the taste and smell of the spray carried on the wind and the periodic apparition of rainbows. You will think you have the entire vista in sight when you begin Gullfoss, but will discover a new level and fall at each step. This double waterfall can be appreciated in all seasons—at the heigh of its power in summer or surrounded by ice that glints in the winter sun. When the falls are covered by fog or obscured at night, its haunting rumble is even more thrilling, fascinating and frightful. *From Gullfoss, 4x4 vehicles can continue on to Hveravellir by the path of Kjölur, the most-trod of the Highlands. To head back towards the south, turn around and then turn left on Route 30 (in direction of Selfoss).* **Route 30** soon crosses the river Hvítá, not far from the site of **Brúarhlöð,** where it finishes crossing the narrow ravine it has followed since Gullfoss. It's here, near the natural pillars nicknamed "the giant and the giantess", that the first (wood) **bridge** over the Hvítá was constructed in 1906, in preparation for the visit of the king of Denmark, Frederick VIII, the following year.

Addresses

Skateboarding outside Harpa
© Ragnar Th. Sigurdsson/age fotostock

🍴 *Where to eat*

The capital offers a range of cafés and restaurants. Across the board, lunch menus offer significantly better value for money.

☺ Restaurant kitchen closes at 10pm.

🕯 *Find the addresses on our maps using the numbers on the listing (e.g. ①). The coordinates in red (e.g. D2) refer to the detachable map (inside the cover).*

REYKJAVÍK

Feeding yourself

To keep costs down, many visitors use the kitchen in the place where they're staying. You'll findfind **supermarkets** in every area. **Bónus *E4*** *(Laugavegur 59 - Mon-Thu 11am-6.30pm, Fri 10am-7.30pm, Sat 10am-6pm, Sun 12pm-6pm)* offers the best prices. Certain branches of the more expensive **10-11** *(10am-11pm)* are open 24 hours, such as those in Austurstræti *C3* and Laugalækur *Off map by H3* (near the campsite). Well-supplied **bakeries** in the town center include **Bernhöftsbakari *D3*** *(Klapparstíg 3 - 8am-5pm/6pm)* or **Sandholt *D4*** *(Laugavegur 36 - 7.30am-6pm, w/e 8am-5pm)* and, near the camp site, **Kornið *Off map by H3*** *(Laugalækur - 7.30am-5pm)*. For an **organic grocery store**, head for **Frú Lauga *Off map by H3*** *(Laugalækur 6)* near the camp site.

68

Less than 3 000 Kr

② **Bæjerins Betzu** – *C3* - *Tryggvagata 1 - ☏ 511 1566 - www. bbp.is - Sun-Thu 10am-1pm, Fri-Sat 10am-4.30pm - 450/650 kr.* Featured in movies, on TV, and often referenced in thrillers, this hot dog kiosk is the best-known in the country. An ideal spot to discover the national favorite, the pýlsur.

⑯ **Sea Baron Sægreifinn** – *B2* - *Geirsgata 8 - ☏ 553 1500 - www. saegreifinn.is - 11.30am-8pm - 1 350/3 500 kr. reserv. 4 pers. mini.* Formerly a sort of greasy spoon frequented by fishermen, this restaurant now attracts a number of tourists, drawn by the irresistible aroma of lobster bisque. You will also find skewers of fresh fish, served grilled with potatoes.

⑩ **Hamborgarabúlla Tómasar** – *B2* - *Geirsgata 1 - ☏ 511 1888 - www.bullan.is - 11.30am-9pm - 990-1 790 kr - menu (burger + fries+ drinks).* The neighbor of no. 16 (above), this pocket-sized Art Deco building, crowned with its own little clock is rarely empty, and for just cause: the burgers on offer are juicy and delicious. An institution!

⑤ **Mýrin Mathus** – *C6* - *Vatnsmýravegi 10 - ☏ 552 1288 - www. myrinmathus.is - ♿ - 7.30am-9pm - 1 690/2 990 kr.* The cafeteria of the terminal of the BSÍ bus serves hearty, good-value fare. Unbeatable portion size for your buck for the fish of the day, burgers and mutton stews served with soup, salad and coffee.

🍴

6 Eldsmiðjan – D5 -
*Bragagata 38a - ☏ 562 3838 - www.
eldsmidjan.is - 11am-11pm - from
1675 kr. Takeaway menus from
1995 kr.* The wood-oven pizzas draw
dedicated fans to this quiet little
corner house. Another address at
Laugavegur 81.

17 Café Loki – D5 - *Lokastígur 28 -
☏ 466 2828 - www.loki.is -
Mon-Sat 9am-9pm, Sun 11am-9pm -
1 750/3 200 kr.* The patrons of this
cafe spill over onto the pavement
in summer; the upstairs room with
a view over Hallgrímskirkja is also
popular. Choose from a number of
Icelandic dishes concocted with a
base of a tasty bread and toppings
(herrings, cured meat, eggs) or a
more substantial dish of the day
(lamb chop, fish balls, fish stew).

14 Kaffivagninn – B2 -
*Grandagarði 10 - ☏ 551 5932 - http://
kaffivagninn.is - ♿ - 7.30am-9pm -
☕ (weekdays). 7.30am-11am, w/e
9am-11am) 450/1 790 kr, brunch
(w/e 11.30am-4pm) 2 690 kr, lunch.
(11.30am-4pm) 2 490/2 990 kr.* In this
unpretentious port café, diners feed
on garnished hunks of bread, soup
and other simple dishes. Picturesque
atmosphere and pleasing view over
the fishing boats.

25 Salka Valka – D4 -
*Skolavördustigur 23 - ☏ 571 1289 -
9am-10pm - 1 200/3 000 kr.* An
impeccable welcome and a manifestly
open atmosphere: expect a very
international staff, a huge map of
Iceland on one wall and a map of the
world on the other. On the menu are
a range of sandwiches and simple but
tasty fish-vegetable dishes.

24 Mat Bar – D3 - *Hverfisgata 26 -
☏ 788 3900 - www.matbar.is -
12pm-11pm - midday 1 250/2 850 kr;
evening 1 840/2 890 kr.* The
management of this bar-restaurant,
opened in early 2017, decided to
marry Italian and Nordic flavors.
Tapas are on offer, with a big choice
at under 2 000 kr - a rare luxury in
Iceland these days *Menu: 8 plates of
tapas 6 940 kr.*

22 Hverfisgata 12 – D3 -
*Hverfisgata 12 - ☏ 437 0203 - www.
hverfisgata12.is - 5pm-11pm; Fri
4pm-1am, Sat 11.30am-1am, Sun
11.30am-11pm - pizzas 2 450/3 450 kr.*
The entrance of this stunning hidden
treasure is deliberately unremarkable,
almost disguised in fact. There are
three rooms on the first floor where
you can enjoy delicious pizzas,
washed down with cocktails or one
of twenty draft beers. Then there
are two more maze-like floors, with
a distinct dolls house feel, offering a
unique and intimate atmosphere.

From 3 000 to 6 000 Kr

13 Icelandic Fish & Chips – C2 -
*Tryggvagata 11 - ☏ 511 1118 - www.
fishandchips.is - ♿ - 11.30am-9pm -
1 390/6 190 kr.* Expect well put-
together fresh and simple ingredients
in this organic bistro. Here, the dish of
the day is accompanied by potatoes
and a selection of original sauces.
Delicate salads balance it all out.

3 Apotek – C3 - *Austurstræti 16 -
☏ 551 0011 - http://apotekrestaurant.is
- ♿ - Mon-Thu 11.30am-11pm, Fri
11.30am-12am, Sat 12pm-12am, Sun
12pm-11.30pm - 1 690/5 990 kr;
menu w/2 courses 3 390 kr, menu w/*

70

3 courses 4 390 kr. Expect luxurious yet cool design credentials and a wide cocktail menu, plus an ideal central location to stay and enjoy Argentinian fare from chef Carlos Gimenez.

⑮ Sólon Bistro – *D3* - *Bankastræti 7a - ℘ 562 3232 - www. solon.is - Sun-Thu. 11am-11.45pm Fri.-Sat 11am-1am, ⌣ - brunch (8am-2pm) 1 990/5 200 kr.* This café-bistro is a safe bet. It's a touch trendy but not intimidating: walkers in Gore-Tex can happily stop in and enjoy a salad, risotto, burger or fish of the day. Jazz at the back.

④ Café Paris – *C3* - *Austurstræti 14 - ℘ 551 1020 - www.cafeparis.is - ₺ - 8.30am-10pm, Fri-Sat 8.30am-11pm - 2 400/5 600 kr - lunch menu 1990 kr.* An institution with a strategic placement, this is a great spot for lunch, brunch or a "coffee-newspaper" in the morning. The salads, breads, and international dishes are a little expensive and, frankly, not outstandingly tasty, but they are served in a pleasant indoor space or on the terrace which is entirely overrun on sunny days.

☺ ⑦ - Grillmarkadurinn – *C3* - *Laekjargata 2A - ℘ 571 7777 - www. grillmarkadurinn.is - ₺ - Mon-Thu 11.30am-2pm, 5.30pm-10.30pm, Fri 11.30am-2pm, 5.30pm-11.30pm, w/e 5.30pm-10.30pm - 2 190/7 790 kr, tasting menu 10 900 kr.* Exceptional design reigns here, with artfully blended lava stone, basalt and woods. The counter in the lower room, constructed like a suspension bridge, is itself worth the visit. The menu is comprised primarily of dishes made from local farm ingredients.

Our recommendations: the rhubarb mojito to start and the gourmet fish (fish trio) as a main dish.

⑨ Laekjarbrekka – *C3* - *Bankastraeti 2 - ℘ 551 4430 - http://laekjarbrekka.is - ₺ - 11.30am-11.30pm - at midday, dish 2 900-3 300 kr, menu 3 courses 3 690 kr; evening, dish 4 300-6 400 kr, menu 4 dishes 8 500 kr (13 500 kr with wine).* With its black panelling and red roof, it's hard to miss this little house which invites a visit. Intimate and warm ambiance. The must-tries: fishes of the day and lobster.

⑱ Þrir Frakkar – *D5* - *Baldursgata 14 - ℘ 552 3939 - www.3frakkar.com - ₺ - Mon-Fri 11.30am-2.30pm, 6pm-10pm, w/e 6pm-11pm - 1 350/6 250 kr - midday 2 750/4 690 kr.* At the "Three French", the sea spray jumps right out of the plate! In a pretty house (1919) divided into little rooms, the fish of the day is prepared in Icelandic style or finished nouvelle cuisine style. Expect traditional and stereotypical fare: reindeer, mackerel and guillemot eggs in season.

⑫ Höfnin – *C2* - *Geirsgata 7c - ℘ 511 2300 - www.hofnin.is - Sun-Wed 11.30am-2pm, 5pm-10pm - 2 990/5 290 kr, lunch menu 2 450/3 400 kr, other menu 8 350 kr.* Set in one of the pretty green houses on the port is this welcoming space (terrace on the dock) where you can savour fine fish dishes, plates of mussels and inventive desserts.

㉑ Geiri Smart – *D4* - *Hverfisgata 30 - ℘ 528 7050 - www.geirismart.is - 11.30am-2pm,*

6pm-10pm, Fri 11.30am-2pm, 6pm-10.30pm, Sat 6pm-10.30pm, Sun 6pm-10pm; w/e brunch 12pm-2pm - midday 2 200 kr, menu 2 950 kr; evening menu 2 courses 5 500 kr, 5 courses 10 900 kr; brunch 2 950 kr. The well-thought-out décor happily marries blue velours and gold-toned lighting, with copper lamps and superb ceramic-covered columns. Rectangular central counter and view of kitchen. The pretty decent dishes use original products with a varied provenance, evidenced in the interesting menu. Very relaxed bistro feel upstairs.

20 Vox – **H5** - Suðurlandsbraut 2 - ☏ 444 5050 - www.vox.is - &. - 11.30am-10.30pm - lunch menu (11.30am-2pm) 3 950 kr or à la carte 2 990/5 200 kr - brunch (Sat 11.30am-2pm, Sun 11.30am-3pm) 4 200 kr, evening menu 8 900/10 900 kr or à la carte 4 500/6 490 kr. On the ground floor of the Hilton, this restaurant, which offers a changing seasonal menu, is a sort of shop window of Nordic nouvelle cuisine. A very popular brunch.

11 Skolabru – **C3** - Pósthússtræti 17 - ☏ 511 1690 - www.skolabru.is - &. - 5pm-10pm - 3 900/7 600 kr, discovery menu 3 courses 6 600/7 600 kr. A beautiful 1906 family house that was transformed into a restaurant in the middle of the 20C. Expect three rooms across two levels and raw food gastronomy. You can choose from a range of original specialties, such as goose carpaccio. There's an Indian restaurant on the lower-ground level.

From 3 000 to 12 000 Kr

8 Fishmarkaurinn – **C3** - Aðalstræti 12 - ☏ 578 8877 - www.fiskmarkadurinn.is - entry 3 200/3 600 kr, dish 4 800/7 200 kr (langoustines 9 900 kr), tasting menu 11 900 kr. Interiors are all fine woods and the food is executed with taste, too: expect a refined blend of local meats and fishes and Asian influences. An emblem of the vitality of Icelandic nouvelle cuisine.

23 KOL Restaurant – **D5** - Skólavördustígur 40 - ☏ 517 7474 - http://kolrestaurant.is - 5.30pm-10pm, Fri-Sat 5pm-11pm - starter 2 890/4 190 kr, main 4 690/8 990 kr; 3 course menu 8 390 kr, gourmet menu 9 490 kr, tasting menu 9 990 kr. Intimate atmosphere with interiors embellished with wood and leather. A flavor-filled menu is on offer spanning seafood, steak and cheesecake. The bar is a great spot to prop yourself with a drink, too.

19 Dill – **D3** - Hverfisgata 12 - ☏ 552 1522 - http://dillrestaurant.is - reservations - Wed-Sat - 6pm-9.15pm - wine-food pairings 5 courses 9 900 kr, 7 courses 11 900 kr. Unmistakably Nordic! From the furnishings to the dishes prepared by star chef Gunnar Karl Gíslason, pioneer of Icelandic nouvelle cuisine, everything here is proudly Scandinavian.

The set menus comprised of a number of small dishes—ultra-fresh fish, wild game flavored with mountain herbs, inventive desserts—that pay homage to the architect of this site, Alvar Aalto.

Dish of fish and potato

IN HAFNARFJÖRÐUR

In the 'city of lava', you will find in Strandagata, a **bakery** (*8am-5.30pm, w/e 4pm*) and, at n° 9, the sweet café **Súfistinn** (*8.15am-11.30pm, from 10am on Sat and 11am Sun*).

Less than 3 000 Kr

Gló – *Laugavegur 20b - Hafnarfirði - ☏ 553 1111 - www.glo.is - 11am-9pm - 1 690/2 390 kr.* At the heart of Hafnarfjord, you'll find this restaurant with its bright, modern décor blending white, wood and flowers. The influential Solla Eiríksdóttir is the face of raw food in Iceland, a trend focused on staying as close to the raw product as possible, which has been heartily adopted by a new generation of chefs. It is sourced from local farms, but also uses more exotic products. Excellent vegetarian dishes and a varied buffet (soups, fresh fruit, tasty bites, spicy chicken, etc.). Other branch in Reykjavik (*Engjateigur 19 - ☏ 553 1111*).

REYKJANES PENINSULA

KEFLAVÍK

Nettó supermarket in the center of Keflavík and **Bónus** at the end of Njarðabraut, at the entrance of Njarðvík.

🍴

Less than 3 000 Kr
Olsen Olsen – *Hafnargata 62 - ☎ 421 4457 - www.olsenolsendiner.com - ♿ - 11am-10pm - 990/2 795 kr.* A journey back to 1950s America and a total calorie overload!

From 3 000 to 6 000 Kr
Kaffí Duus – *Duusgata 10 - ☎ 421 7080 - http://duus.is - ♿ - 11am-10pm - 2 850/7 500 kr.* A large selection of well-prepared fish, served in a friendly environment. Great cakes for dessert and fine view of the sea.
Ráin – *Hafnargata 19 - ☎ 421 4601 - www.rain.is - ♿ - 11am-1am, Fri-Sat 11am-3am - 1 940/4 990 kr.* Neighbour of the above; a retro space with a seaside location. Classic cuisine, though a little expensive.

SANDGERÐI

From 3 000 to 6 000 Kr
Vitinn – *Vitatorg 7 - ☎ 423 7755 - www.vitinn.is - ♿ - daily except Sun 11.30am-2pm, 6pm-9pm - 950/5 250 kr - menu 6 850/9 600 kr.* After visiting the Nature Center, why not stop in here to try out a specialty crab dish?

GRINDAVÍK AND THE BLUE LAGOON

Guaranteed port atmosphere in Grindavík: local crowd and kitsch rock groups on Friday evenings.

Less than 3 000 Kr
SjómannastofanVör – *Hafnargötu 9 - ☎ 426 8570 - www.grindavik.is - 11.30am-1pm - 1200 kr.* For a meal on a budget, try the lunch buffet.
Bryggjan – *Miðgarður 2 - ☎ 426 7100 - ♿ - 7am-11pm - 1 100/2 000 kr.* A place to stop on the port to grab soup, sandwich or cake.

From 3 000 to 6 000 Kr
Salthúsið – *Stamphólsvegi 2 - Grindavík - ☎ 426 9700 - www. salthusid.is - ♿ - 12pm-10pm (winter 9pm) - 1 500/7 600 kr.* For more elaborate fare after a visit to the Saltfish Museum, try the specialties at Salthúsið. In this large chalet,close to the football stadium whose fine grandstand is the envy of many other localities on the island, tuck into nicely prepared fish.

More than 6 000 Kr
Lava – *Nordurljosavegur 9 - Blue Lagoon - ☎ 420 8800 - www. bluelagoon.com - ♿ - 11.30am-9pm - 4 590/5 900 kr - lunch menu 2 courses 6 400 kr, 3 courses 7 600 kr, evening menu 4 courses 10 300 kr.* The restaurant looks on to the basin and serves excellent fusion dishes using Icelandic produce.

THE GOLDEN CIRCLE
Most voyagers visit the Golden Circle in one day. Stand-alone restaurants are more rare and generally attached to lodgings.

LAUGARVATN

The **Samkaup** supermarket *(9am-6pm, Sat 10am-6pm, Sun 11am-6pm)* offers hearty previsions at low prices. Well-stocked little shop at the **service station**, which also offers burgers.

From 3 000 to 6 000 Kr

Lindin Restaurant – *Lindarbraut 2 - ℘ 486 1262 - www.laugarvatn.is - 12pm-10pm - 2 200/2 480 kr, set menu 6 300/8 950 kr.* This is without a doubt one of the best restaurants of the region. Wood floors, tablecloths, flowers and chandeliers welcome—as does a fine view over the lake—as diners enjoy delicious local cuisine. Well prepared reindeer, lake char, guillemot, goose, partridge and lobster bisque served in generous portions won't fail to entice. Reservations recommended at the weekend.

GEYSIR

Beyond the restaurant of the Geysir hotel (♿ p. 88), you'll find a little café-boutique and a restaurant in the **Geysir Center** (♿ p. 62).

Less than 3 000 Kr

Geysir Glima – *Haukadalur - ℘ 481 3003 - http://geysirglima.is - ♿ - 10am-5pm - 1 590/2 690 kr.* An immense restaurant of excellent quality located alongside the boutique at the Geysir Center. Large stone tables or little wooded corners, with an idiosyncratic 'vintage' touch: videos of the Icelandic struggle of the last century playing on loop. Tasty snacks and respectful service, even during the busiest hours.

GULLFOSS

Less than 3 000 Kr

Gullfoss Kaffi – *Gullfossi Bláskógabyggð - ℘ 486 6500 - http://gullfoss.is/cafe - ♿ - 10am-7pm - 770/1 550 kr.* There is a vast café-restaurant by the entrance of the site. Delicious lamb soup (1950 kr) and simple dishes (salads, sandwiches, meat and potatoes) are laid out for self-service.

AROUND FLÚÐIR

There is a **Samkaup** supermarket *(Mon-Fri 10am-6.30pm, Sat 10am-7pm)* close to the Icelandair Hotel Flúðir.

Less than 3 000 Kr

Kaffi Sel – *Efra-Sel - Efra-Sel (3 km to the north of Flúðir) - ℘ 486 6454 - http://kaffisel.is - 11am-9.30pm - 1 100/4 190 kr - 6 rooms - 19 300/14 700 kr.* Set up in the golf club house, the Kaffi Sel serves soups, pizzas and international dishes in a pleasant atmosphere.

VALLEY OF ÞJÓRSÁ

Árnes is the only supply point in the valley. Levillage offers **service station-cafeteria N1**, which has a shop.

75

Where to drink

The Icelandic capital is proud of its collection of cafés, which can also double as restaurants and clubs.
👌 *Find the addresses on our maps using the numbers on the listing (e.g. ➊). The coordinates in red (e.g. D2) refer to the detachable map (inside the cover).*

REYKJAVÍK

Cafés/Bars

➊ **Stofan Kaffihús** – *C3* - *Vesturgata 3 - Arrêts de bus: Stjórnarráðið, Ráðhúsið, MR - 𝒫 546 1842 - www.facebook.com/ stofan.cafe Mon—Wed. 9am-11pm, Thu-Sat 9am-12am, Sun 9am-10pm - 780/2 490 kr - happy hour 3pm-9pm: pint 750 kr; glass of wine 950 kr.* A historic establishment, formerly located in a delightful little yellow house on Astravollur square, now located just next door to it. The space is laid out across two levels decorated with exposed brick and stylishly mismatched décor (vintage armchairs and leather couches). A haven for local hipsters and the height of Icelandic chill.

➋ **Ölstofan** – *D4* - *Vegamótastígur 4 - 𝒫 552 4687 - www.facebook.com/ OlstofaKormaksogSkjaldar - 3pm-1am, Fri-Sat 4am.* A pub so discreetly tucked away you may have trouble finding it. Interiors are dark yet welcoming, with a central oval-office style bar; large choice of whiskies and an exclusive local draft beer (Brio).

➌ **Kaffismiðja** – *D4* - *Kárastígur 1 - 𝒫 517 5535 - www.kaffismidja.is - 7.30am-5pm, Sat10am-5pm, Sun 10am-4pm.* A hidden little address, that delights coffee lovers. Grains are chosen by the coffee-enthusiast owner and blended on site in pretty pink machines. Enjoy your cup at one of the little tables.

➍ **Smurstöðin** – *D2* - *Austurbakka 2 - 𝒫 519 9750 - www. smurstodin.is - 10am-6pm, w/e 11am-6pm.* Pick up a juice, coffee, a dessert or a Franco-Danish style tasty bistro dish and enjoy the location in the heart of the magnificent Harpa. Outdoor terrace in summer.

➎ **Babalú** – *D4* - *Skólavörðustígur 22a - 𝒫 555 8845 - ♿ - 9am-11pm.* The mural-covered facade sets the tone for the cool café inside. Expect bright colours, a charming hodgepoge of furnishings and, crucially, good coffee and delicious cakes. Exhibitions on the ground floor.

➏ **Haítí** – *C2* - *Geirsgata 7b - 𝒫 588 8484 - www.cafehaiti.is - ♿ - 6am-6pm, w/e 7am-6pm - ☕ 1 790/2 500 kr - lunch 1 350/ 2 990 kr.* Housed in one of the emblematic green houses on the port, this unpretentious address is a great spot to stop in for a coffee or beer—or a salad, sandwich or dessert.

Enjoying drinks on a terrace of a bar

7 Kaffibarinn – *D4* - *Bergstaðastræti 1 - ℘ 551 1588 - www. facebook.com/kaffibarinn - Sun.-Thu 3pm-1am, Fri-Sat 3pm-4.30am - 650/1 000 kr.* This bohemian café, which doubles as a haunt for night owls at the end of the week, featured in the film *Reykjavík 101*. Young and laid-back clientele; indie-rock music.

8 Mokka – *D4* - *Skólavörðustígur 3a - ℘ 552 1174 - http://mokka.is - 9am-6.30pm - 1000 kr.* One of the capital's first cafés feels practically unchanged since its beginnings in 1958.

9 Holt – *C5* - *Bergstaðastræti 37 - ℘ 552 5700 - http://holt.is - 4pm-11.30pm.* The soundtrack is gentle and unobtrusive, fitting with the understated feel of this plush and understated café-lounge, housed inside a luxury hotel. Here you'll find well-off tourists, not-struggling artists and local celebrities rubbing shoulders over a drink while contemplating the Kjarval canvas above the bar.

Shopping

In the town center, the scarcity of international brands means the experience of shopping is guaranteed to feel distinctly Icelandic. **Laugavegur** and **Bankastræti** *C3/C5* (fashion, outdoor, jewelery), **Skólavörðustígur** *D4* (design, jewelery, artisan goods) and the area around **Ingólfstræti** *D3/C4* house the majority of shops to visit.
The city is also served by two **shopping centers**: **Kringlan** *(Kringlunni - bus 1, 2, 4)* and **Smáralind** *(Kópavogur - bus 2)*.
♿ *Find the addresses on our maps using the numbers on the listing (e.g.* ❶*). The coordinates in red (e.g. D2) refer to the detachable map (inside the cover).*

78

REYKJAVÍK

Flea market
❶ **Kolaportið Flea Market** – *C3* - *Tryggvagata 19* - ☎ *562 5030* - *http://kolaportid.is* - *w/e 11am-5pm.* In an old port market hall is this old-school bazaar, where you can peruse books and knitwear, as well as typical Icelandic food products. Even if you don't bag any bargains, the atmosphere makes this well worth a visit.

Wool and fashion
❷ **Geysir** – *D4* - *Skolavordustigur 16* - ☎ *519 6000* - *http://geysir.com* - ♿ - *10am-7pm, Sun 11am-6pm.* Icelandic and Scandinavian leather and clothes. High prices to match the cool factor.

❸ **Handknitting Association of Iceland** – *D4* - *Skólavörðustígur 19* - ☎ *445 5544* - *http://handknit.is* - *9am-6pm, Sun 12pm-6pm.* Gloves, socks, hats and sweaters knitted by a dedicated association.

Álafoss – *Off map* - *Álafossvegur 23* - *Mosfellbær (15 km/9mi to the north of the city, route n°1)* - ☎ *566 6303* - *www.alafoss.is* - *8am-8pm, w.-end 9am-8pm.* This wool-everything shop is established on the spot where the wool industry began.

❺ **Dogma** – *D4* - *Laugavegur 39* - ☎ *562 6600* - *www.dogma.is* - *10am-6pm, Fri 10am-6.30pm, Sun 1pm-6pm.* Indie screenprinted T-shirts and prints.

❻ **Kron** – *E4* - *Laugavegur 48* - ☎ *551 8388* - *http://kron.is* - *10am-6pm, Sat 10am-5pm - closed Sun.* A shoe shop long-frequented by Icelandic fashion-lovers.

⓱ **Farmers & Friends** – *D4* - *Laugavegur 37* - ☎ *552 1960* - *www.farmersmarket.is* - *10am-6pm, w/e 11am-5pm.* Opened in May 2017 in an old fish factory. All-natural-fabric clothing and accessories so you can look like an impeccably cool and stylish farmer. A huge range of local products; perfect interior decoration.

Design, jewellery and accessories
❾ **Gullkúnst Helgu** – *D4* - *Laugavegur 13* - ☎ *561 6660* - *www.gullkunst.is* - *10am-6pm, Sat 10am-4pm - closed Sun* An exceptionally charming jewelry boutique right in the center of town.

There's a piece to suit every taste at Gullkúnst: matte, sparkling or both in one piece. The shop also creates made-to-measure pieces and can adapt its offering depending on client's request.

⑦ Kraum – *D3* - *Bankastræti 7a - ☎ 517 7797 - & - 11am-6pm, Sat 11am-5pm - closed Sun.* Chocolate volcanoes, jewelry, handmade glasses and knit stools, ceramics: here you'll find a selection of creations from 200 local artisans, set in one of the oldest houses in the city.

⑧ Aurum – *C3* - *Bankastræti 4 - ☎ 551 2770 - http://aurum.is - summer: 10am-10pm, Sat 10am-6pm, Sun 12pm-5pm; rest of the year: 10am-6pm, Sat 11am-5pm, Sun 1pm-5pm.* It's hard to resist this silver jewelry inspired by Icelandic nature.

Atson – *Off map by H7* - *Súðarvogur 32 - ☎ 699 6029 - http://atson.is - Mon-Thu 1pm-3pm.* Since 1936, this boutique has specialized in leather accessories and other products using animal, like fish skin, for example.

Outdoors and camping
As a result of its bracing climate, various Icelandic makers produce all-weather and all-terrain clothing; it's (very) expensive but of very high quality.

⑪ Zo-On Iceland – *D3* - *Bankastræti 10 - ☎ 527 1050 - http://zo-on.is - 10am-6pm, Sun 1pm-6pm.*

⑫ 66° Nord – *C3* - *Bankastræti 5 - ☎ 535 6680 - www.66north.com - 9am-8pm, Sun 10am-8pm.*

Farmers Market – *Off map by C1* - *Hólmaslóð 2 - ☎ 552 1960 - www.farmersmarket.is - 10am-6pm, Sat 11am-5pm - closed Sun*

⑭ Útilíf – *H8* - *Kringlan 4-12 - Kringlan shopping center - ☎ 545 1530 - www.utilif.is - & - Mon-Wed 10am-6.30pm, Thu 10am-9pm, Fri 10am-7pm, Sat 10am-6pm, Sun 1pm-6pm.* Your place if you need any camping supply.

Books, souvenirs, antiques
⑮ 12 Tónar – *D4* - *Skólavöðustígur 15 - ☎ 511 5656 - www.12tonar.is - 10am-6pm, Sun 12pm-6pm.* Both music shop and indie label, you have everything you need here to discover the richness of the Icelandic scene. Listen in the shop and choose sometime to take home.

⑯ Arctic photo – *E4* - *Laugavegur 64 - ☎ 695 3536 - www.arcticphoto.is - Mon-Fri 10am-6pm, Sat 10am-5pm.* The work of Örvar Thorgeirsson is far from traditional photography, with the use of retouch and editing bringing it closer to painting. Purists may not approve of the process, but the skill is undeniable.

👁 For a more realistic homage to the country's beautiful landscapes, look to the work of artists such as the legendary Ragnar Axelsson, known as **Rax**, who creates stunning black and white shots *(www.rax.is)*; see also the surgical precision of the photos of **Palmi Bjarnason** and **Sigrun Kristjans-dottir** *(www.iceland image.com)*.

Nightlife

Check *Grapevine (http://grapevine.is)* and *What's On (www.whatson.is)*.
♪ Find the addresses on our maps using the numbers on the listing (e.g. ①). The coordinates in red (e.g. D2) refer to the detachable map (inside the cover).

REYKJAVÍK

Cafés, bars, clubs

Seemingly low-key cafés transform into wild party spots at the end of every week, attracting dancers, solid drinkers and music-lovers (of

different genres). Together, they create and facilitate the tradition of *rúntur* (♪ *p. 25*). **Kaffi Sólon**, the "legendary" **Kaffibarinn** and **Vegamót**, the favorite address of local youth (playing R&B, hip hop).

① **Prikið – *D3* -** *Bankastræti 12 - ℘ 551 2866 - http://prikid.is - 8am-1am, Fri 8am-4.30am, Sat 11am-4.30am, Sun 11am-1am - 1 390/3 990 kr.* This quiet and well-established café (more than 60 years old) is frequented by arty young people. It transforms at the end of the week into a temple for all-nighters with hip hop and R&B in a Guinness-soaked atmosphere.

② **Boston – *D4* -** *Laugavegur 28b - ℘ 571 5781 - www.facebook.com/ boston.reykjavik - 2pm-1am, Fri-Sat 2pm-3am.* A welcoming spot where you'll find patrons of all ages. Expect a warm ambiance jazz and oldies played at acceptable volume; even on a Friday night, you can hear the other people at your table, or your companions on the dance floor.

③ **Hressingarskálinn (Hressó) – *C3* -** *Austurstræti 20 - ℘ 561 2240 - www.hresso.is - 10am-1am, Fri-Sat 10am-4.30am- 1 990/4 890 kr.* A trendy Icelandic spin on a 1950s American diner, with the added bonus of courtyard, a great spot on a warm day. The address attracts crowds during rúntur. Sounds of the moment and occasional live acts.

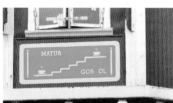

© aimintang/iStockphoto.com

Prikið

© Ragnar Th. Sigurdsson/age fotostock

Harpa during Children's Cultural Festival

④ Lebowski Bar – *D4* -
Laugavegur 20b - ☏ *552 2300* -
www.lebowskibar.is - ♿ - *11am-1am,*
Fri-Sat11am-4am - closed Mon -
890/2 750 kr. Site entirely dedicated
to the cult Coen brothers film. Menu
is themed around the characters: you
can choose from The Other Lebowski
burger or The Nihilists chicken wings.
Very, very lively during wee hours at
the weekends.

Shows
⑤ Harpa – *D2* - *Austurbakki 2* -
☏ *528 5000* - *www.harpa.is* - ♿ -
8am-12am. The home of the Iceland
Symphony Orchestra and the
Icelandic Opera. Touring international
stars and English-language
comedians perform here.

**⑥ Þjóðleikhúsið (National
Theatre)** – *D3* - *Hverfisgata 19* -
☏ *551 1200* - *www.leikhusid.is* - ♿ -
closed Jul-Aug - tickets 12pm-6pm.

Cinema
Among the city's several cinemas, it's
worth highlighting the following:
⑦ Bíó Paradis – *D4* -
Hverfisgata 54.The most central.
⑧ Háskólabíó – *A5* - *Hagatorg* -
www.haskolabio.is. On University of
Iceland campus. Varied programme
covering art films.
Multiplex – In the shopping centers
of Kringlan (Kringlunni 4 - bus 1, 2, 4)
and Smáralind (Kópavogur - bus 2).

Where to stay

If you are a light sleeper, avoid accommodation in the city center on Friday and Saturday nights. In summer, be sure to bring an eye mask to counteract the inefficacy of local curtains.

☺ Try to reserve your hotel several months in advance if you are visiting in summer. In low season, hotel rates fall by between 30 and 50 %.

☀ Find the addresses on our maps using the numbers in the listing (e.g. ❶). The coordinates in red (e.g. D2) refer to the detachable map (on the inside cover).

REYKJAVÍK

Less than 10 000 Kr

Reykjavík Eco Campsite – *Off map by H3* - Sundlaugavegur 32 - Bus 14, stop: Laugardalslaug - ℘ 568 6944 - www. reykjavikcampsite.is - ♿ - showers available 24h, use of kitchen free, car rental and excursion booking, shuttle service to Langmannlaugar - 900 spaces - 2 000/2 400 kr/pers. depending on duration - ☕ 1650 kr - 🍴. Located 2.5/3 km/ 1.5/1.6mi from the center, in the area of Laugardalur, this camping benefits from the facilities of the neighboring youth hostel: bike rental, computers, washing machines, kitchen, barbecue, wifi, showers, etc.

Reykjavík City Hostel – *Off map by H3* - Sundlaugavegur 34 - Bus 14, stop: Laugardalslaug - ℘ 553 8110 - www.

hostel.is - ♿ - 174 dorm beds 4 350/6 050 kr/w/bath ; private rms. (2-4 pers.) 19 300/30 600 kr w/bath - ☕ 1600 kr - possibility of booking rooms w/3 to 8 beds, sheets included. Next to the camp site (above), this is a modern, comfortable, fun (activities, films, games) hostel. You will find kitchens, a laundry room, cloakroom, and bikes for hire, and you can easily arrange trips and excursions at reception.

⑰ Reykjavík Downtown Hostel – *B3* - Vesturgata 17 - Bus 14 stop: Mýrargata - ℘ 553 8120 - www. hostel.is - 68 dorm beds 6 000/ 8 650 kr ss/with bath; dbl room 21 500/27 200 kr ss/with bath - ☕ 1600 kr. This hostel has got everything going for it: a central location, pleasant décor, café, great kitchen, laundry room and welcoming communal spaces.

From 20 000 to 40 000 Kr

Most addresses in this category are **guest houses** (GH) of which many close in winter, or house students.

⑩ Sunna Guesthouse – *D5* - Þórsgata 26 - Hlemmur shuttle available from the airport - ℘ 511 5570 - http://sunna.is - 52 rooms. - 19 950/32 900 kr w/ bath - ☕ from 7am-9.30am. At the foot of Hallgrímskirkja, in a quiet and colorful little area, this very well-kept guest house offers practical, functional rooms.

7 Butterfly Guesthouse – *B3* -
Ránargata 8a - 10min by foot from the town center - ☏ 894 1864 - http:// butterfly.is - 6 rooms - 19 000/22 500 kr w/bath ☐ - 2 apartments (2-4 people) 29 900/37 500 kr. In a green house set on a quiet road in the old town are a few slightly worn but charming and spick and span rooms.

3 Álfhóll Guesthouse – *B3* -
Ránargata 8 - 10min by foot from the town center - ☏ 898 1838 - www. alfholl.is - 9 rooms - from May-Sep - 19 900/24 900 kr w/ bath ☐. Neighbor of the above. Quality facilities and welcoming staff.

13 Metropolitan Hótel – *B3* -
Ránargata 4a - 2minby foot from the central square - ☏ 511 1155 - www. metropolitan.is - 30 rooms - 23 900 kr ☐. This modest hotel offering basic comforts (small rooms, bathroom, TV) enjoys a fine position on Ránargata road; quiet and friendly.

19 Three Sisters – *B3* - *Ránargata 16 - 2 steps from Laugarvegur shopping center - ☏ 565 2181 - www. threesisters.is - from mid-May to the start of Sep - 16 studios (2 people) 22 700 kr.* A number of studios spread across two vast buildings close to the port. Inoffensive décor, decent beds, practical kitchenettes.

8 Óðinsvé – *D4* - *Þórsgötu 1 - 5minby foot from the town center - ☏ 511 6200 - www.hotelodinsve.is - 50 rooms - 36 000/40 000 kr ☐ - TV - ✗.* In a quiet and central area, where each house is painted a different color, this charming hotel is noteworthy for its comfortable Scandinavian-style rooms. Pleasant bistro with washed wood décor (Franco-Icelandic kitchen).

5 Icelandair Hotel Reykjavik Marina – *B2* - *Mýrargata 2 - Accessible by Flybus from the airport - ☏ 444 4000 - www.icelandairhotels.com - ♿ - computer access - 147 rooms - 33 745/45 645 kr ☐.* In 2012, this port building was converted into an unusual hotel. The ground floor, with a large lobby and lounge, is divided into a number of open spaces with relaxation rooms, a cinema area and gym. It mixes concrete, wood, and wool with cushions and floral wallpaper.

16 Alda Hotel – *E4* -
Laugavegur 66-68 - ☏ 553 9366 - www.aldahotel.is - 88 rooms 36 400/40 100 kr - ☐ 2 600 kr. A discreet, almost hidden, entrance belies the superb hotel inside, which succeeds better than any other in mixing elegance and sobriety (it's often one or the other in Iceland). Fairly spacious rooms with all the comforts and decorated in attractive shades of grey.

From 40 000 to 60 000 Kr

11 Klöpp – *D4* - *Klapparstígur 26 - In the heart of the town center - ☏ 595 8520 - www.centerhotels.com/ klopp-2 - 46 rooms - 40 000/44 400 kr ☐ - private bathroom, TV, minibar - ✗ 17 200/40 100 kr ☐ - 7am to 10am.* Scandinavian décor and comfort in this fine establishment that rounds the corner of a street below Laugavegur. In the rather small rooms, expect polished parquet, light and warm colors on the walls and bedspreads and contrasting dark slate in the bathrooms. In upper levels, a beautiful view over the bay.

④ **Holt** – **C5** - *Bergstaðastræti 37 - ☎ 552 5700 - http://holt.is - 42 rooms - 42 450/48 800 kr 🍽 - ✗.* Behind an unremarkable facade hides unexpected décor featuring wood, plush carpet and deep armchairs. This retro luxe hotel houses one of the country's largest private art collections. The bar, complete with fireplace, is dangerously welcoming (it's hard to leave) as is the excellent restaurant. Rooms are appealing with comfortable furnishings, original paintings, etc.

⑮ **Radisson 1919** – **C3** - *Pósthússtræti 2 - ☎ 599 1000 - www.radissonblu.com - ♿ - 88 rooms - from 37 000 kr 🍽 - ✗.* Opened in the 2000s in the former harbour master's office, this fine establishment combines very Scandinavian modern comforts and historic communal spaces, brought out with the contrast of contemporary sculptures.

② **Arnarhvoll** – **D3** - *Ingólfsstræti 1 - ☎ 595 8540 - www.centerhotels.com/hotel-arnarhvoll/- ♿ 104 rooms - 43 000/47 000 kr 🍽 - ✗.* The austere lines of this building house Scandinavian-design rooms. Breakfast served in a room on the roof with a view over the bay, the port and neighboring Harpa.

⑥ **Borg** – **C3** - *Pósthússtræti 11 - Shuttle available from the airport - ☎ 551 1440 - www.keahotel.is - Spa, gym ,wifi - 42 435/49 900 kr 🍽 - ✗.* An Art Deco building dating from the1930s on the principle square of the capital. You'll find luxurious salons and rooms furnished with modern comforts. Founded by a famous fighter, the Borg is one of the most well known historical hotels in Iceland. The 43 rooms, decorated in beige-brown tones, do not enjoy the direct view of Austurvöllur square.

㉑ **Þingholt** – **C4** - *Þingholtsstræti 3-5 - ☎ 595 8530 - www.centerhotels.com/hotel-thingholt/- Bar, spa, meeting rooms, computers - 52 rooms - 45 300/52 275 kr 🍽 - ✗ - wifi.* Icelandic nature inspired the modern design of this charming hotel located right in the city center. Handsome colors and materials, and irreproachable service.

⑭ **Kvosin Hotel** – **C4** - *Kirkjutorg - ☎ 571 4460 - www.kvosinhotel.is - 24 rooms - 31 000/73 000 kr.* Probably the most beautiful facade in Reykjavik. Large rooms with light parquet (a change from the usual grey wood flooring found in Reykjavik). Trendy copper-decorated bar across two levels. Seven versions of gin & tonic and more than 40 varieties of whisky.

More than 60 000 Kr

㉓ **101 Hotel** – **D3** - *Hverfisgata 10 - Accessible by Flybus from the airport - ☎ 580 0101 - http://101hotel.is - 38 rooms - from 51 000 kr 🍽.* This was one of Iceland's first design hotels when it opened in 2004, and far from being outdated, it continues to play a part in conferring the status of Reykjavík as a trendy travel destination. You'll find wood interiors with touches of glass, open fires, sculptures and cozy eider duvets in the rooms: the perfect spot for a secluded, indulgent and luxurious stay.

🛏️ **⑫ Canopy by Hilton** – **D4** - *Smidjustígur 4 - ☎ 528 7000 - http://canopy3.hilton.com - 115 rooms - from 63 200 kr.* The layout of this hotel is like a labyrinth, with two entrances on two different levels and a choice of staircases to get to the bar (also on two levels) and the restaurant (Geiri Smart, see "*Where to eat*"). Very well thought-out designs in the rooms.

REYKJANES PENINSULA

KEFLAVÍK AND NJARÐVÍK

Less than 10 000 Kr

Fit Hostel – *Fitjabraut 6b - Njarðvík - ☎ 421 8889 - www.fithostel.is - 29 rooms - 6 900/7 900 kr, sleeping bag 3 000 kr.* A clean, well-equipped hostel, with a convenient location close to facilities.

From 20 000 to 40 000 Kr

Guesthouse 1x6 – *Vesturbraut 3 - Keflavík - ☎ 857 1589 - www.1x6.is - 6 rooms - from 18 500 kr - ☕ 2 500 kr - one shared bath per floor (3 rooms/floor).* Rooms are decorated with maritime elegance by local artist Daniel Hjötur Sigmundsson. Welcoming communal spaces and an enchanting stone hot pool in the middle of the garden.

Keilir – *Hafnargata 37 - Keflavík - ☎ 420 9800 - www.hotelkeilir.is - 40 rooms - 26 400 kr - ✗.* Located in the old town is this hotel with modern rooms with a sea view.

Berg – *Bakkavegur 17 - Keflavík - ☎ 422 7922 - www.hotelberg.is - ♿ - 36 rooms - 27 000/31 000 kr - ☕ 2 500 kr - ✗.* An American-style

house with comfortable rooms and a view over the port.

Airport Hotel Aurora Star – *Blikavöllur 2 - Keflavíkurflugvöllur - ☎ 595 1900 - www.hotelairport.is - ♿ - 73 rooms - 30 200/35 200 kr ☕ - ✗.* A brand new chain hotel; not much character, but practical.

From 40 000 to 60 000 Kr

Hôtel Parkinn by Radisson – *Hafnargata 57 - Keflavík - ☎ 421 5222 - www.parkinn.com - ♿ - 81 rooms - from 41 000 kr ☕ - ✗.* A good location in the town center; cozy little Scandinavian-design rooms.

VOGAR

From 20 000 to 40 000 Kr

Hótel Vogar – *Stapavegur 7 - ☎ 866 4664 - www.hotelvogar.is - ♿ - 35 rooms - 22 000/27 000 kr ss/with bathroom ☕.* In the heart of a little coastal village between Keflavík and the Blue Lagoon is this motel, offering good value for tourists traveling by car. Rooms comfortable and well proportioned. Kind welcome. Breakfast served in a room with a touch of kitsch. No restaurant, but there's a pleasant pizzeria opposite.

GRINDAVÍK AND BLUE LAGOON

Less than 15 000 Kr

Camping – *Hausturvegur 6 - As you enter town, go around the roundabout and head straight along Víkurbraut. Turn left at Ránargata and left again at Austurvegur (near*

the church) - ☎ 660 7323 - www.
visitgrindavik.is - mai-nov. - 1800 kr/
per. In the heart of this port village is
this the most beautiful campsite of
the peninsula.

Guest House Borg – *Borgarhraun 2 -
Grindavík - ☎ 895 8686 - www.
guesthouseborg.com - 7 rooms.
ss bathroom - 15 000 kr 🖵.* Large red
house with clean and pleasant rooms
and comfortable communal spaces.
Kitchen, laundry facilities, internet—
and a warm welcome.

From 20 000 to 40 000 Kr

Northern Light Inn –
*Norðurljósavegur 1, Northern Lights
Road - Shuttle available from the
airport - ☎ 426 8650 - www.nli.is -
♿ - 32 rooms - from 33 900 kr 🖵 - ✗.*
Two paces from the Blue Lagoon,
the vast and welcoming rooms here
look onto the lava or the basin of the
lagoon. Free shuttle to airport; good
restaurant.

More than 60 000 Kr

Silica Hotel – *Nordurljosavegur 9 -
Blue Lagoon - ☎ 420 8800 - www.
bluelagoon.com - ♿ - 35 rooms -
67 000/70 000 kr - 🖵 - ✗.* A
bright hotel in wood and lava glass,
integrated into the peak. The very
comfortable rooms please, as do the
spa treatments on offer.

THE GOLDEN CIRCLE

Most visitors cover the Golden Circle
in a day, before continuing on their
journey or going back to Reykjavík.
Campsites and a handful of hotels
are on offer for those who do wish to
linger in the region.

ÞINGVELLIR

Since the only hotel caught on
fire, the camp site is the single
accommodation option within the
national park.

Less than 10 000 Kr

Camp sites – *Austurstræti 12 -
☎ 482 2660 - www.thingvellir.is - ♿ -
Jun-Sep - 1600 kr/pers* Two sites on
offer: close to the Information Center
and fault lines, four sites on offer for
all kinds of campers with showers
nearby; 3 km/1.8mi farther, secluded
on the edge of the lake on the site of
the former farm at Vatnskot (tents
only, rudimentary toilet block).

From 20 000 to 40 000 Kr

Skálabrekka – *Heiðarás,
Thingvallasveit - Set away from Route
36, 5 km/3.1mi from Þingvellir -
☎ 892 7110 - www.lakethingvellir.is
- 4 chalets Jun-Aug - 19 500 kr
(+ 2 500 kr/pers.) - 2 nights min.* The
chalets dominate the lake. Ideal for
tourists traveling by car.

LAUGARVATN

Less than 20 000 Kr

Youth hostel – *Dalbraut 10 -
☎ 486 1215 - www.laugarvatnhostel.is
- ♿ - 140 beds - Feb-Nov -
dormitory 5 300 kr, double room
13 300/15 800 kr ss/with bathroom -
🖵 1700 kr.* Three well-equipped
buildings (cute little house or vast
school complex), close to the edge
of the lake and near facilities. Various
accommodation options, from
dormitory to family rooms. Hot tub
and laundry room.

Edda ML – *Laugarvatn - ✆ 444 4810 - www.hoteledda.is - ♿ - 101 rooms - from start of Jun to mid-Aug - 12 900/19 650 kr w/bath - ☒ 2 400 kr -* ✘. Two buildings at the entrance of Laugarvatn house large rooms with boarding-school-style décor; some have sinks and bathrooms.

From 20 000 to 40 000 Kr

Edda Íkí – *Laugarvatn - ✆ 444 4820 - www.hoteledda.is - ♿ - 28 rooms - from start of June to end of August - 29 650/36 000 kr - ☒ 2 400 kr -* ✘. Same student accommodation feel as above. All the rooms have bathrooms. Half offer fine views over the lake and Hekla.

Efsti-dalur II – Farm Hotel – *Efstidalur II - Laugartnsvegur - ✆ 486 1186 - http://efstidalur.is - 10 rooms - from 22 000 kr* ☒. This farm between Laugarvatn amd Geysir has been transformed into a rather pleasant guest house. Diner possible in summer. Hot tub.

GEYSIR

Less than 20 000 Kr

Geysir Camping – *Haukadalur - ✆ 480 6800 - www.geysircenter.is - ♿ - from mid-May to mid-Sep - 1700 kr/pers -* ✘. The site is fairly rudimentary, but located just two steps from the geysers and facilities.

Hótel Geysir – *Haukadalur - ✆ 480 6800 - www.geysircenter.is - ♿ - 77 rooms - 13 900/17 300 kr - ☒ 1400 kr -* ✘. Some of the pleasant rooms here look directly onto the geothermal area. The restaurant

also enjoys a fine view and serves Icelandic and international cuisine, a buffet at midday *(11.30am-2pm)* and an evening menu *(2 800/5 950 kr)*. A range of activities on offer (pool, horse riding, etc.).

GULLFOSS

From 20 000 to 40 000 Kr

Hótel Gullfoss – *Blaskogabyggd - Bratthol (500 m/164 ft on the right before Gullfosskaffi) - ✆ 486 8979 - www.hotelgullfoss.com - ♿ - 35 rooms - 26 000/31 200 kr - ☒ -* ✘. The greatest draw of this hotel is its position on the edge of the Hvítá. It's rather expensive and not particularly charming, but the rooms are decent. Restaurant with Icelandic cuisine with fine views. Hot tub.

AROUND FLÚÐIR

Less than 20 000 Kr

Camping – *Skeida og Hrunamannavegur - Gata 5 - Flúðir - ✆ 618 5005 - www.tjaldmidstod.is - ♿ - May-Sep (w/e and on reservation in May and Sep) - 1 500/1 750 kr.* Situated in the heart of the locality, on the riverside, this well-equipped campsite (toilet block, laundry, TV) is popular in summer with inhabitants of the capital, who come here to relax or (noisily) party.

Guest House Saga – *Syðra-Langholt - Syðra between Flúðir and Laugarás, Route 340 - ✆ 772 1299 - www.guesthousesaga.is - 12 rooms - 16 000 kr* ☒. This farm arranged around a large white house offers

Camping in the Southern Region

space for campers and has different types of rooms. Warm welcome, invigorating hot pool. Horseback excursions.

From 20 000 to 40 000 Kr

Icelandair Hotel Flúðir –
Vesturbrún 1 - Flúðir - ℘ 486 6630 - www.icelandairhotels.com - 🦽 *- 32 rooms - from 24 390 kr* 🛏 *-* 🍴. A fine hotel with rows of rooms arranged under pointed roofs and pretty and light communal areas. Views over the surrounding areas.

ÞJÓRSÁ RIVER VALLEY

Less than 20 000 Kr

Sandártunga camping ground –
Sandártunga, Þjórsárdal - ℘ 893 8889 - http://tjalda.is - 🦽 *- from mid-May to end of August - 1500 kr/ pers.* Not far from Stöng, amid a beautiful pine forest, you'll find this rustic campsite, which enjoys an exceptionally secluded position .

Steinsholt – *Steinsholt II - Steinsholt - Hruni - ℘ 486 6069 - www.steinsholt.is - 8 rooms - from 10 100/13 500 kr ss/ with bathroom* 🛏 *-* 🍴. Built set back from a beautiful landscape, this horse farm houses rudimentary rooms decorated in warm tones. Hot tub and horseback rides.

Planning Your Trip

Know before you go

Taking pictures on Krýsuvíkurberg cliffs, Reykjanes Peninsula
© Ragnar Th. Sigurdsson/age fotostock

Know before you go

ENTRY REQUIREMENTS

See **www.mfa.is** and **www.iceland.is/iceland-abroad/fr**.
Documents – EU, US, Canadian, Australian and New Zealand citizens can stay for up to 90 days. A valid passport is required (must be valid three months before the end date of your planned trip).
Iceland is part the Schengen Zone and as such there are no border checks for flights coming from other member countries.
Customs – You cannot bring **fresh produce** into Iceland (including meat, dairy, eggs).
The import of other food products is capped at 3kg.
Those 18+ are permitted to import one carton of **cigarettes**, and those over 20 are permitted to bring1 liter of alcohol and 1 liter of wine.
Fishing equipment that's been used outside of Iceland (including boots) is prohibited. ✆ www.tollur.is.

TO REYKJAVIK BY PLANE

Airport
Keflavík Airport – ✆ *425 6000* - *www.isavia.is*. 50km/31mi to the west of the capital.

Regular airlines
Icelandair – www.icelandair.com. Iceland's national airline, of which each plane is named after a volcano.
SAS – www.flysas.com

Low-cost airlines
Transavia – www.transavia.com.
WOW – www.wowair.fr.
Norwegian – www.norwegian.com

MONEY

The Icelandic currency is the *króna*, or *krónur* in plural; international code ISK. In this guide we use the abbreviation **kr**.
Beyond the (slightly cumbersome) coins of 1, 10, 50 and100 kr, there are also notes for 500, 1000, 2,000 and 5,000 kr. Iceland is expensive.

Money exchange
Money can be changed in banks (in all towns) and exchange windows in the capital and at the airport. Exchange rate can varys.
⊘ The Icelandic króna is not exchangeable, so avoid bringing any home.

Bank cards
All towns have ATMs that accept international cards. Icelanders use cards for any and all transactions, from a coffee to a night in a hotel.
⊘ Note whether your card charges a foreign transaction fee.

SEASONS

Changing, capricious and often surprising, the climate is influenced by the **Gulf Stream**, which maintains cool temperatures in summer (10-20°C) and moderately cold temperature

is the winter (0 to -5 °C, dipping to -15 °C at night in the central deserts). The **humidity** and **wind** are the most disturbing elements.
🔊 http://en.vedur.is – Information on the (tricky) weather forecasts.
The **high tourist season** runs from mid-June to the end of August. This is the ideal time to make the most of the country's outdoor activities and all the island has to offer, as everything is open and running. Booking your trip well in advance is key. Prices are also (unsurprisingly) at their highest during this period. The summer season now tends to stretch from **the end of May to the end of September**. In these shoulder periods, some facilities are closed, but visitors can enjoy a bit of quiet, and conditions are favorable for whale- and bird-watching. The period between **October and April**, which can be grey and rainy, suits those wishing to visit the capital, as well as winter skiers. This is the period for spotting the **Northern Lights** in the night sky.

FIND OUT MORE

Tourist brochures:
www.inspiredbyiceland.com.
🔊 *Tourist information, p. 98.*
www.nat.is – Independent site (Nordic Adventure Travel) dedicated to tourism in Iceland.

EMBASSIES

Canadian Embassy– *Túngata 14 -* 📞 *(354) 575 6500 - www. canadainternational.gc.ca/iceland-islande.* The Canadian embassy

provides assistance to Australians.
US Embassy– *Laufásvegur 21 -* 📞 *(354) 595 2200- is.usembassy.gov*
British Embassy– *Laufásvegur 31 -* 📞 *(354) 550 5100- www.gov.uk/ world/organisations/british-embassy -reykjavik*

SHOPPING/TAXES

Make sure you get reimbursed for the (high) VAT on the products labeled *tax-free* in the shops (in airport departure hall). You need both receipts and a **form that you will need to have asked for** at the time of purchase. The tourism office offers a brochure entitled *Where to shop tax-free in Iceland*, which lists all the relevant locations.
🔊 http://premiertaxfree.com

ALCOHOL

Beyond the local beer, which is refreshing in summer but lacking a little in character, the national alcohol is **brennivín**, a schnapps flavoured with caraway.
A prohibition on beer was imposed between 1915 and 1989 and Icelanders celebrate the removal of the ban every year on March 1, an anniversary that has earned the name **Beer Day**; the lost decades are made up for during **rúntur** that weekend! There are still some strict rules: no drinking and driving (naturally) and no selling alcohol to anyone under 20. In addition, the selling of alcohol is still **a state monopoly**, and you will only find (very) mild beers in the supermarket. Other alcoholic drinks

can only be bought in designated state-run shops, called **vínbúðin**; queues outside these establishments are impressive at the end of the week, despite the exorbitant prices! The prices encourage drinkers to consume everything they buy, including party guests and visitors!

CRAFTS AND ARTISANS

Icelandic Mountain Guides offers "knitting and trekking" trips.
👣 www.mountainguides.is

HITCHHIKING

Though it is not particularly reliable as a sole mode of transport, hitchhiking works well on the most frequented roads, especially at the weekends. Service stations are the most obvious spots. Bear in mind that hitchhiking always entails risk, even in a country as safe as Iceland.

SWIMMING AND THERMAL BATHS

Don't count on swimming in the sea, except in the tepid waters of Reykjavík's Geothermal Beach. Iceland does, however, have several hundred hot springs, which serve the **public pools** (water at 27°C and *hotpots* between 36 and 42 °C) or **natural bassins** in the middle of the desert, some of which are still closely guarded secrets. Splashing around in the pool at Laugardalslaug (👣 p. 33) à Reykjavík is an unfailing favorite and taking a dip in the milky waters of the Blue Lagoon a necessity. There

are many other sites besides where you can share in Icelanders' favorite past time.
👁 For hygiene reasons, you should, before bathing in any of the pools, thoroughly wash your whole body Signs (and pool attendants) are there to remind you, too.

BUS

Bus companies charge high prices, but they offer a **comprehensive network** and adhere to the advertised timetables.
Pick up a copy of the **timetables** (*Iceland on your own!*), which is updated annually and available at BSÍ (*see below*), in tourist offices and at the airport. Outside of Reykjavík station, **stops** are made in the bus stations of the main towns or in front of service stations.

Network and companies
BSÍ Terminal – *Vatnsmýrarvegi 10* - 📞 *580 5400* - *www.bsi.is* - *4.30am-12am*. Reykjavík's bus station is located to the south of Lake Tjörnin, 10min by foot to the south of the town center or reachable by bus routes 1, 3, 6, 14 and 15. It constitutes the central point of the national network. Tickets and travel cards for all bus companies are on sale on site. There's a cloakroom and a cafe here (👣 *Where to eat, p. 68*).
Strætó – 📞 *540 2700* - *www.straeto.is*. City buses from the capital also provide the Reykjavík-Hveragerði-Selfoss link.
Sterna – 📞 *551 1166* - *http://sternatravel.com*. The largest

company serving the whole country.
Reykjavík Excursions – *BSÍ -
Vatnsmýrarvegi 10 - Reykjavík -
℘ 580 5400 - www.re.is.* Operates
in the south of the country, notably
in the Peninsula of Reykjanes and
the Golden Circle. The company also
specializes in one-day excursions to
major tourist sites.

Tickets and passes

Stræto – Tickets are sold at the
BSÍ, in tourist offices, or aboard the
vehicle (make sure you have the
right amount). Put aside 460 kr for
a ticket, 8 700 kr for a book of 20
or 1700/4 000 kr for a 1-3 day pass.
The Reykjavík City Card gets you
unlimited journeys. (🕭 *See Tourist
offers next page).*

DANGERS

Violent winds, flash floods, thick fog,
and **brutal changes of weather** all
represent real dangers for walkers
(🕭 *p. 99)* and those traveling by car.
Motorists in particular—and especially
those not used to driving a 4x4—
should not take any unconsidered
risks. Everyone is advised to have
a mode of communication on them
at all times, in case of emergency,
and we also advise downloading **the
(free) app 112**, which allows you to
quickly reach emergency services
(with GPS localization) in case you run
into any major problems.
www.road.is – Information on the
state of the roads.
The isle counts some one hundred
active volcanoes whose eruptions
can cause earthquakes, projections of

> ### No need to panic!
> **European emergency number:** ℘ 112
> **Medical emergencies:** ℘ 585
> 1300 (hôpital public de Reykjavík)
> **Lost bak cards:** ℘ 0 892 705 705
> (0,34 €/mn).

lava, lava flows, dust clouds, etc. Make
sure you follow recommendations
offered by the authorities an ro stay
informed.
www.avd.is – Website of Civil
Protection.

ELECTRICITY

Iceland uses standard Northern
European plugs (two round prongs)
requiring adapter types C or F.
Voltage is (50 Hz/220 V).

95

LOCAL TIME

Iceland is in the GMT+ 0 Time Zone, but
there is are no seasonal adjustments,
like Daylight saving time.

OPENING HOURS

Banks and administration – From
Monday to Friday 9am to 4pm.
Shops – From 9am or 10am to 6pm
on weekdays and 10am to 4pm on
Saturday (and until midday for some).
Souvenir shops extend these hours, as
do service stations and supermarkets,
which stay open on Sunday
(sometimes until 11pm, or even 24hrs
in the capital).
Restaurants – Continued service
from 11.30am (earlier for cafés) to

9pm-10pm. If the establishment doubles as a bar, service continues to 1am, or even 3am on the weekend.

TOURIST OFFERS

Reykjavík City Card – *http://visitreykjavik.is. Valid 24hrs : 3 800 kr; 48hrs: 5 400 kr; 72hrs: 6 500 kr - 6-16 years 1600 kr.* This card includes admission to museums, pools and urban transport in the capital, as well as reductions in a selection of shops, on some excursions, bicycle hire etc. On sale at the tourist office, the BSÍ, participating attractions and some hotels.

TOURIST INFORMATION

Present in every locality (only open in summer outside of the big cities), the tourist information booths are a must. Along the roads, a number of little car parks offer signs detailing historic events and geological phenomena.

In Reykjavík

Tourist Information Center – ♿ *See p. 14.* A must-visit. A huge number of brochures and literature covering culture and practical advice for the capital and the rest of the country. Also: Internet access, Tax Free kiosk, money exchange, excursion and hotel booking, plus **Reykjavík City Card** purchase (♿ *Tourist offers, above*). See also;

Icelandic Travel Market – *Bankastræti 2 - ☎ 522 4979 - www.icelandictravelmarket.is - Jun-Aug: 9am-8pm; rest of the year: 9am-7pm.*

In Reykjanes Peninsula
Grindavík – ♿ *See p. 50.*
Blue Lagoon – ♿ *See p. 48.*
Keflavík Airport – ♿ *See p. 3.*

In the Golden Circle
Þingvellir Information Center – ♿ *See p. 56.*
Geysir Center – ♿ *See p 62.*

INTERNET

Icelanders are well set-up for internet, so you won't find many cybercafés. You will, however, find internet hot spots (sometimes at a charge) in youth hostels, tourist offices and libraries. There is generally a Wi-Fi connection on buses and in cafés and hotels.

PUBLIC HOLIDAYS

Shops and administrative centers are closed on public holidays.
Christmas – From the afternoon of the 24 to the 26 December.
New Year – 31 Dec and 1 Jan.
Easter – From Maundy Thursday to Easter Monday.
Summer Festival – The 3rd Thursday of April or the first Thursday following 18 April.
Labour Day – 1 May
Ascension Day – In May or June depending on the year.
Whit Monday – In May or June depending on the year.
Icelandic National Day – 17 June.
Merchants' Weekend – 1st or 2nd Monday of August.

LANGUAGE

The archaic and preciously preserved **Icelandic** is the national language. Nearly all natives speak **English**, especially those working in tourism. With only a few exceptions, you will get along fine speaking English, but taking the time to learn and use a few Icelandic words is always appreciated.

LAUNDRY

In a country with a temperamental climate, where a walk is often a humid and muddy affair, laundry facilities can prove very useful! Washing machines (at a charge) and sometimes dryers are on offer in campsites and youth hostels. Allow between 500 and 1000 kr.

MEDIA

Local media

Iceland sits at the top of the world rankings for freedom of the **press**. A number of daily newspapers share this market of keen readers, including **Morgunblaðið**, **DV** and **Fréttablaðið,** which are among the best-selling. Visiting tourists may wish to consult **Iceland Reviews** (http://icelandreview.com) and **Grapevine** (http://grapevine.is), two mines of information on Icelandic society and cultural news and updates.

On **television**, alongside satellite channels, **Stöð 2**, **Skjár 1** and the public **RÚV**, formerly Sjónvarpið, diffuse local news and subtitled American programs. A program made for kids went the opposite way : *LazyTown (Latibær)* has been sold in 100 countries. This is a rapid cultural revolution for Iceland which, up until 1988 only had one channel, which stopped broadcasting from Thursday evening until Monday!

MUSEUMS

From the art galleries and historical museums of the capital to eccentric little spaces hidden beyond a fjord and run by amateurs, there is no shortage of museums in Iceland, nor lack of variety. Whether they are dedicated to herring fishing, a local painter, geothermics, or indeed the penis, they collectively transmit the **cultural dynamism** of the country, as well as Icelanders' characteristic passion for their history and particularities. To participate in the hugely successful tourism industry, a number of small towns and localities are investing in their cultural heritage. **Prices** – From 500 to 1500 kr, free for children and reductions for students and retirees.

WHALE WATCHING

Icelanders not only hunt and consume whales but also offer whale watching as an activity; both industries are lucrative.

Between April and October, different cetacean species (dolphins, blue whales, humpback whales and more rarely blue whales) can be observed (which species depends on the month). Observation boats leave from Reykjavík, Hafnarfjörður and Keflavík.

See **www.icewhale.is** for info on species and seasons.

In Reykjavík

The capital is flooded with ads from a number of companies, whose kiosks you'll find on the pier ofÆgisgarður. **Elding** (*☎ 519 5000 - http://elding.is*), is the leading company and offers up to six outings a day between June and August; **Whales Safari** is another significant player (*☎ 497 0000 - www.whalesafari.is*). Allow around 11 000 kr for the excursion.

ORNITHOLOGY

From the sharp warning cry of the oystercatcher to the sad whistle of the golden plover (👣 *p. 62),* the sound of birds will accompany all your walks in Iceland. In fact, Iceland is a veritable paradise for lovers of aerial fauna. You can explore on your own, binoculars in hand, heading for the best observation sites. Otherwise, local agencies can also provide guides. **www.birds.is** – List of agencies and services, information on birds: passage, nesting and locations.

NATIONAL PARKS

Beyond its natural reserves (Lake Mývatn, Surtsey, Flatey, Fjallabak, etc.) Iceland also has three national parks. Described in this guide, **Þingvellir National Park** (👣 *p. 56*) was created in 1930 and is listed by UNESCO. It protects the historic Alþing. The other two are the **Snæfellsjökull National Park** (www. snaefellsjokull.com), covering 170km^2

/65mi2 including a section of sea and protecting the tip of the Snæfellsnes Peinsula. **Vatnajökull National Park** (www.vatnajokulsthjodgardur.is), inaugurated in 2008, is a new addition; it is the largest in Europe (12,000 km$^{2/}$ 4633m^2). It was created to counterbalance the construction of the dam in Kárahnjúkar, in the east of the country

UNESCO SITES

Þingvellir National Park (👣 *p. 56)* has been listed as a World Heritage site by Unesco since 2004.
Reykjavík enjoys a reputation as a literary town.
Other sites, such as Vatnajökull, Lake Mývatn where the turf-roofed houses are waiting to be listed.
👣 http://unesco.org

POLITENESS AND CUSTOMS

Only a few decades ago, Icelanders were stunned to discover any foreigners visiting their island, where the living conditions are so stark. Today, they are both concerned by and used to their *Gore-Tex*-sporting visitors; tourism is a financial godsend but has its ecological drawbacks. If Icelanders can at first seem a little distant, fear not; you'll gain their confidence and be warmly welcomed by being pleasant and respectful.
In Icelanders' homes – It's customary to remove your shoes when visiting someone's home.
Respecting laws– Sticking to the rules is expected of citizens and visitors alike. The police force is discreet and

friendly, but they keep a close eye out.

Gender equality – Iceland ranks first for gener equality. Male chauvinism is not exercized here, and overtly macho behaviour will not please locals.

Tips – Very rare in Iceland. The practice is not customary here, but a tip won't be refused.

Toilets – Toilets (generally pay toilets) are signposted and well mantained in the cities and tourist sites.

POST OFFICE

Post offices are open Monday to Friday from 9am to 4pm. In Reykjavík, they close at 6pm and some stay open on Saturday. **www.postur.is**

WALKING

From casual strollers to sporty types, Iceland offers walking options to cater for every taste and level. The instability of the climate is part of the thrill, as there are always surprises in store in the island's varied and rich landscapes: lava fields, majestic fjords, black sand deserts, isolated beaches, fearsome glaciers, monumental cliffs, hidden hot springs...the list goes on!

Walking in Iceland must be synonymous with **respect**: for the fragile natural environment you must be careful not to disturb; for the weather whose mood swings should never be underestimated; and for the local rules, which may sometimes feel draconian but are justified. In other words, a successful walk on the island of volcanoes must be planned! Fortunately, the established **walking routes** make the logistics easier, with their accompanying rest spots, guides, camp sites and transport to and from the routes.

In July and August, the walking routes are the victim of their own success, which means you'll need to book ahead to stay in the little guesthouses along the way (often monopolized by agencies), and the magic of the most popular sites can be marred a little by the crowds. Walking in May, June and September, however, should allow for relative 'exclusivity'.

Safe hiking

– Make sure your insurance covers accidents.

– Never leave the established tracks, in order to preserve the environment and to avoid natural hazards (crevasses, fault lines, etc.).

– Don't disturb the piles of stones, as these are used as place markers.

– Be sure to keep up to date on weather conditions.

– Leave no rubbish or trace.

– Tell the owners of your guest house and even other walkers where you're planning to walk.

– Make sure you're appropriately prepared for the cold, wind and humidity. Your shoes should be strong, impermeable and flexible in order to adapt to the changing terrains (crumbly lava, sand, mud etc.). A stick is useful for gauging the deepness of the river when you cross fjords. A good map, a compass, binoculars for bird-watching, water, and some snacks will also need to be added to your bag (which should of course be waterproof).

99

Walking on Viðey Island

Around Reykjavík
The periphery of the capital offers some opportunities for pleasant walks.
Peripheral walks, p. 34.

Reykjanes Peninsula
Criss-crossed by a number of walking paths.
www.nat.is

HEALTH AND EMERGENCIES

Precautions
Vaccinations – No particular vaccinations are required.
Venomous insects and animals – There are no venomous snakes or reptiles on Icelandic soil. Mosquitoes and wasps are an occasional nuisance, as are swarms of midges in summer, which begin to disappear at higher altitude. Look out for ticks in grassy areas.
Water– Water is potable everywhere, even if it sometimes gives off a pronounced odour of sulphur. Avoid drinking water from mountain streams and waterfalls if you know there are sheep grazing upstream (possible parasites).

Insurance, medical treatment
If you are eligible for one, bring your **European Health Insurance Card** (request at least 15 days before departure) and purchase travel insurance (covering hospitalization and repatriation).
Pharmacies (*apótek*) – Same opening hours as shops. Some open nights and weekends.

Doctors – The FCO website (*www.gov. uk/government/publications/iceland-list-of-medical-facilitiespractitioners*) recommends a list of doctors. For emergencies, the public hospital of Reykjavík (*Landspítali - ☏ 543 1000*) is the most signposted. All towns have a free clinic (Heilsugæslustöð - www. heilsugaeslan.is).
☏ *No need to panic, p. 104.*

SOUVENIRS

Wool

Known for its length, quality and softness, *lopi* (Icelandic sheep's wool) is the base of a lively enthusiasm for knitting. The very warm **Icelandic sweater** (*lopapeysa*), with its traditional motifs, is worn by locals across the country. Its effectiveness is due to the combined use of internal wool (flexible, soft and insulating) and external wool (thick and impermeable due to its natural oils). (Rather expensive) sweaters, gloves and socks are sold n souvenir shops and artisan craft shops, as well as some farms.

Outdoor items

Icelanders have become masters in the making of all-weather clothing. Local brands such as 66° North, Cintamani and Zo-On Iceland have carved out a well-deserved international reputation.

From lava, to bone, to skin

Icelandic artisans, artists and designers skilfully employ local materials (driftwood, bones, animal and fish skin, lava) to create lamps, clothes and jewelry. Nature also provides various ingredients which are used to make organic cosmetics.

Gastronomy

Smoked fish, dairy produce, liquorice confectionery and, of course, the legendary **brennivín** (☏ *p. 93*), make interesting souvenirs despite import restrictions.
www.shopicelandic.com – Online store of Icelandic products.

SPORTS

Beyond **walking** (☏ *p.99*) and **cycling** (☏ *p. 103*), Icelandic nature also offers a number of sports and activities.
☏ http://.adventures.is.
☏ If you're planning on participating in adventure sports, make sure the activity is covered by your insurance (☏ *p. 100*).

Horse riding

Icelanders hold an affection for their famous **Icelandic horse**. Though it's still used by some farmers to herd sheep, its function is primarily **recreational**. Many farms and travel agents run short excursions or long treks on horseback. All riders, from beginners to confirmed knights, will find a course to suit them.
Near Reykjavík – Íshestar - ☏ *555 7000* - *www.ishestar.is*; **Laxnes** - ☏ *566 6179* - *www.laxnes.is*.
In the Reykjanes Peninsula – From March to October, horseback excursions with **Arctic Horses** (*Grindavík* - ☏ *848 0143* - *www. facebook.com/arctic.horses*).
In the Golden Circle – Various farms

run horseback outings (signposts on the side of the road). One example is **Geysir Hestar** (☎ 847 1046 - www.geysirhestar.com) near Geysir. **Geysir Hotel** (🕯 p. 88) also organizes excursions.

Climbing and mountaineering

Climbing and walking on glaciers requires a guide.

🕯 www.fi.is, www.mountainguides.is **www.insidethevolcano.com** – You can also discover the 'underside' of volcano Þríhnúkagígur near the capital.

Golf

Icelanders have been passionate about this activity for several decades. The courses—65 across the island including 15 and 18 holes—are often to be found in magnificent locations.

www.golficeland.org – List of courses and clubs.

Snow and ice

The country has plenty of peaks, but they are not well-adapted or equipped for **alpine skiing**. The practice is nonetheless possible and pleasant on the edges of the towns or in less frequented sites. In winter, there is skiing on the edges of the capital, at **Bláfjöll** (http://skidasvaedi.is). In theory, **Nordic skiing** can be practiced everywhere.

Glacier hiking (in summer) is also very popular, with beginners and those more experienced; popular sites include Sólheimajökull (for a day trip starting from Reykjavík).

🕯 www.fi.is ; www.mountainguides.is

Fishing

Trout and **salmon** fishing in mountains streams and glacial lakes is a local passion that enthusiasts the world over come to share. The short season runs from April or June to September. A **salmon permit** is very expensive. 🕭 The import of fishing material is forbidden or strictly regulated to avoid any contamination.

www.fishpal.com – Info on species, sites, seasons, rules etc.

www.mast.is – Permits, hygiene.

www.fishingiceland.com – Fishing trips.

Diving and water sports

Diving in Iceland? It is indeed possible, in the incredibly clear glacial waters of the crevasse of **Lake Silfra** (🕯 p. 57) in Þingvellir. Beginners as well as experienced divers can don their masks and kit and move between two continents! Alternative site: the oceanic site of Garður (🕯 p. 46).

SDS Iceland – Hólmaslóð 2 - Reykjavík - ☎ 578 6200 - www.dive.is. This provider organizes one-day excursions leaving from Reykjavík. There's a tempting range of activities on offer: from **rafting** in the torrents that hurtle down from the glaciers to more famiy-friendly **sea kayaking** in the fjords and running along the cliffs. With strong demand, the market for these activities is developing all the time. Excursions, including transport to the site, equipment and even accommodation are offered by most of the specialist adventure sport agencies in Reykjavík.

Caving

It's possible to organize caving excursions in the lava tunnels, notably around Lake Laugarvatn.
Laugarvatn Adventure – ☎ 888 1922 - www.caving.is.

SIGHTSEEING FLIGHTS

The packages are expensive, but in sunny weather the spectacle is undeniably breathtaking.
Atlantsflug – ☎ 854 4105 - www.flightseeing.is.
Helicopter.is Norðflug – ☎ 562 2500 - http://helicopter.is. Flies over Þingvellir, Geysir and Gullfoss.

TOBACCO

Public spaces, restaurants, bars and hotels are non-smoking. A few keep small smoking spaces. It should go without saying that you shouldn't throw your cigarette butts on the ground (Icelanders will send you murderous glances); if you do smoke, make sure you bring a pocket ashtray.

TAXI

Taxi fares are fairly high, but still offer good value for those traveling in groups in capital. Allow around **550 kr** as a base fee and then **400 kr** for every km.
Several companies:
Hreyfill – ☎ 588 5522.
BSR – ☎ 561 0000.
Borgarbíll – ☎ 552 2440.

PHONE

You will still find **phone booths** on the island. They take change; useful for a local call; to call abroad, buy a cards sold in kiosks, post offices, supermarkets and service stations. Mobile phone reception is good in all coastal areas, but uneven, if not absent, in the central desert.
In order to use your phone and pay **local rates**, buy a SIM card, which you can top up in tourist offices and phone shops (including in the airport); try Siminn or Vodafone.

CYCLING

The island is a favorite with brave **cycle tourists** who brave the wind and hop from campsite to campsite. Cycling certainly allows visitors to get up close to Icelandic nature, but the climate, the clouds and the state of the roads makes it an arduous task. Be sure to bring a full repair kit in case of any mechanical problems.
You can also opt to rent a **mountain bike** for a day to explore the area around where you're staying. Rental is on offer in tourist offices, youth hostels farms and guest houses.

In Reykjavík

On a sunny day, despite the wind, Reykjavík is great discovered by bike. Throughout the city, cycle routes stretch along the coastline. Rentals on offer at guest houses, youth hostels, hotels, tourist offices and dedicated bike shops. Allow around 6,000 kr/j.
Reykjavik Bike Tour – Ægisgarður 7- ☎ 694 8956 - http://icelandbike.com.

Bike Company – *Eyjarslóð 3 - ☎ 590 8550 - http://bikecompany.is*.

VISITS AND EXCURSIONS

Information at the tourist office of Reykjavík (✆ *p. 14*): route maps and leaflets describing themed walks (historical , thriller etc.).

Reykjavík Criminality – *http://bokmenntaborgin.is - June-Aug: Thu 3pm - in English - 1hr - free*. The route takes in sites associated with Icelandic thrillers.

⊛ The *Literary Map*, sold in bookshops, allows you to guide yourself on a literary walk through the capital.

Reykjavík Excursions – ✆ *See p. 96*. Departing from Reykjavík, the Blue Lagoon excursion last 1 day; starting from 11,980 kr (including entry to the site).

Golden Circle Excursion, 1 bus/day, year-round, 8hrs, starting from 11,600 kr.

Sterna – *See p. 96*. Circuit round the Golden Circle, in summer, 8am, 12,900 kr.

Gray Line Iceland – ☎ *540 1313 - http://grayline.is*. Starting from Reykjavík-Lækjartorg, a number of excursions are available in the Golden Circle, running 7 days a week and starting from 6,700 kr.

Artic Adventures – ☎ *354 562 7000 http://adventures.is*. This provider offers themed visits of Reykjavík and a number of adventure and disovery excursions in Iceland. Golden Circle, 9am, 11,990 Kr.

CAR

In a country with such a small population, traveling by car affords you a huge amount of freedom. You will, however, want to consider the cost of car rental and gas, the state of the roads and the driving conditions.

✆ *Dangers, p. 95; Driving, p. 105.*

Parking

⊛ In Reykjavík, it's best to opt for the **car parks** the near outskirts of the city, because the car parks in the city are expensive and fines are guaranteed if you forget to pay the old-school parking meters.

Icelandic roads

Route 1, which loops the whole island (1,336km/830mi) is almost entirely tarmacked, but the same cannot be said for the rest of the road network: 15,350 km/9,538mi of roads are covered in asphalt and 9,300km/5,778mi are considered 'track'. Some of the tracks, those that are somewhat covered in earth or gravel, can still be tackled in tourist rental cars. Others can only be driven on by 4x4 and require a certain amount of experience. These dented roads, are qualified as **F-roads** (F for *fjall*), or 'mountain roads' and are only open in summer. This is true of the tracks that cross the center of the island.

The **signposts** are sometimes discreet, but will provide you with a solid **roadmap**, which will tell you how many kilometers you've traveled, the state of the road, the placement of service stations and—on the central roads—the fords and rural huts en route. You will find maps in bookshops and service stations; the **Ferðakort** maps are far and away the best. The GPS offered by car rental companies (at a supplement) can also prove useful. When planning your routes, don't forget that the roads that follow the bends of the fjords or the badly-paved roads take some time to get across.

Info – *www.road.is* - ☎ *1777; www. safetravel.is* - ☎ *570 5929*. Opening dates and state of the road.

Driving

– Speed limit: 50km/hr (31mi/hr) in the city, 80km/hr (50mi/hr) on roads that aren't covered with asphalt roads and 90km/hr (56mi/hr) on others.
– Headlights must be on day and night.
– Between November and April, studded tires are obligatory.
– On bridges and in narrow tunnels, priority is given to the side without side shelters.
– Look out for herds of sheep. If you hit a sheep, you'll have to pay a fine to your rental company and compensation to the farmer. Sound your horn if you see an animal.
– In some places, the wind can blow very strongly and move vehicles.
– On sections of road that aren't covered in asphalt, indicated by the sign *Malbik Endar*, minimize the spray of gravel by slowing down when you encounter another vehicle.
– Driving after any alcohol consumption is forbidden.
– Leaving official roads is forbidden.

Gas

Don't wait for a near-empty tank to fill up. Make sure to identify where the **service stations** are. Often doubling as cafés and mini supermarkets,

these stations are open from 7am until 10pm or 11pm. Outside of these hours, automatic pumps that allow card payments, and sometimes also 1,000 kr notes, do the job.

The (fairly high) **price per liter** doesn't vary depending on the region or proximity to the capital, but rather depending on the brand. You can plan your costs by consulting *www.orkan.is* or *www.n1.is*, a guide to gas brands. ⊘ To avoid paying a commission for each card payment, purchase a prepaid card to the value of 3,000 to 10,000 kr.

Car rental

Car rental comes into consideration for visitors who wish to travel beyond the capital, which itself can easily be discovered on foot. Rental can offer very good value if you're traveling in a group of three or four.

Formalities – In order to rent a vehicle, you must be at least 20 years-old—23 for a 4x4—and have had your license for at least a year.

Tourist car or 4x4 ? – Renting a 4x4 is very expensive. Renting a tourist car will in no way prevent you from getting a good feel for the country, but it will limit your exploration to properly laid roads or only the best tracks. Though some *F-roads* will technically be accessible, in practice the conditions of your car rental will prevent you from taking them. If you decide to infringe the rule, you will not be covered by insurance in case of damage and will be made to pay a hefty fine. If you do opt for a 4x4, make sure you have a clear idea of your rights with the rental company

The Hipster Tour of Reykjavík

FM Belfast is one of many Icelandic groups to have enjoyed international success with a winning brand of electropop ("Mondays" is one of their best-known hits). Band member **Ivar Petur Kjartansson** decided to offer tourists another, less traditional, way to discover his city: "I offer an alternative tour centered around music and food, culture and bars. In particular I like to avoid Laugavegur and Austurstraeti, the two main roads, and instead head down the less-trodden side roads. The idea is to show them the places a musician goes on a typical day. The tour won't particularly suit those who are set on visiting churches and museums," he says. The city's gift shops, complete with stuffed toys, are not on the agenda either. The idea came to Ivar after he noticed there was nothing quite like it on offer. "I speak to everyone as an individual; it's not a guided tour. It's a good way to start your stay here." Note that Ivar is a certified and qualified guide. Make sure you check to see whether he's on tour with his band, somewhere in the world (www.ontourwithivar.com, daily 12.30pm; duration 3hr30min, 11,900 kr).

before you set off and be sure not to overestimate your skills as an all-terrain driver. Some tracks that cross fords are very tricky to navigate and it is wise before attempting these to get information on the road conditions and weather. With all this in mind, many choose to rent a tourist vehicle and then take the bus to the most isolated sites.

Rental companies – Most **international rental companies** are present in Iceland, but it can pay to rent directly from a smaller **local company**, which will generally be less expensive and equally professional. Compare prices, which vary greatly depending on the company and the season. Make sure you're clear on the payment system (deposit or no deposit) and sign up for good insurance, though bear in mind that it will never cover damage to the undercarriage of the car. You can pick up your vehicle in one place and return it in another, at an extra charge; there's also a fee payable for returning the car at Keflavík airport.

Iceland Car Rental – *Arnarvöllur 4 - Reykjanesbær; Knarrarvogur 2 - Reykjavík -* 📞 *(354) 415 2500 - www. icelandcarrental.is*. Availability and attractive prices. The owner offers the same level of service as **Reykjavik Rent A Car** - 📞 *(354) 569 3300 - www.reykjavikrentacar.is/fr.*

Extreme Iceland – *Skútuvogur 2 - Reykjavik -* 📞 *(354) 588 1300 - www.extremeiceland.is/fr.*

Geysir – *Arnarvöllur 4 - Reykjanesbær -* 📞 *(354) 455 0000 - www.geysir.is.*

Atak – *Knarrarvogur 2 - Reykjavík; Blikavellir 3 - Reykjanesbær -* 📞 *(354) 554 6040 - www.atak.is/fr.*

Festivals and events

REYKJAVÍK

March
▶ **Festival of Lights** – *www. foodandfun.is - Feb-start of March.* Festival themed around (naturally) light and also geothermics; special offers in a number of restaurants.
▶ **Beer Day** – *1 March*
▶ **Listahátíð** – *www.artfest.is - end May-start June.* Arts festival (dance, theatre, concerts) in various places across the capital.

June
▶ **Sjómannadagurinn** – *1ˢᵗ w/e of June.* Festival of the sea in a coastal village: banquets, races, sea rescues, etc.

September
▶ **Jazz Festival** – *http://reykjavikjazz.is - start Sep.*
▶ **Film Festival** – *http://riff.is - Sep-Oct.* The best independent films from across the world are rewarded with a golden puffin.

November
▶ **Iceland Airwaves Festival** – *http:// icelandairwaves.is - Oct.* The country's principal pop, rock and electro festival.

HAFNARFJÖRÐUR

June
▶ **Viking Festival** – *Mid-June, 4 days* The town goes back in time.
Ὑ **www.visitreykjavik.is**

REYKJANES PENINSULA

June
▶ **Sjómannadagurinn** – *1st w/e of June.* Fishermen's day, the festival of the sea: street parties, races, sea rescues, etc.

September
▶ **Ljosanott** – *http://ljosanott.is - 1st w/e of Sept* Night of Lights: street party, fireworks, general merriment.

GOLDEN CIRCLE

July-August
▶ **Skálholt classical music festival** – *www.sumartonleikar.is.* Across five weeks in the summer; concerts from Icelandic and international musicians.

Find Out More

109

Ice skating on Lake Tjörnin
© Ragnar Th Sigurdsson@arctic-images.com/Promote Iceland

Key dates in history

COLONIZATION AND THE GOLDEN AGE

8ᶜ – Brief installation of Irish monks.
870-930 – Arrival of the Norwegian Vikings, fleeing the reign of Harald I, the first king of Norway.
Around 871 – Foundation of Reykjavík by Ingólfur Arnarson.
930 – Creation of the Alþing, in Þingvellir, first parliament in Europe.
985-1000 – The banished Erík the Red establishes a colony in Greenland.
1000 – The Alþing votes to adopt Christianity as the official religion.
12ᶜ-13ᶜ. – *Eddas* and Sagas written.
13ᶜ – Violent clashes between clans put the parliamentary model in jeopardy.

UNDER THE DANISH YOKE

14ᶜ – Three major eruptions of the Hekla volcano take place. Norway approaches the Danish crown, which takes control of Iceland.
1397 – Union of Scandinavian kingdoms, isolation of Iceland.
15ᶜ – A plague outbreak kills two thirds of the population.
16ᶜ – Denmark imposes Reform, despite the opposition of the population.

1602 – The king Christian IV establishes a commercial monopoly.
18ᵉ s. – Smallpox, famine and the eruption of Laki (1783) decimates the population.
1800 – Denmark abolishes the Alþing.
Middle of the 19C – The independentist leader Jón Sigurðsson forces Denmark to re-establish the Alþing (1843) and abolish the commercial monopoly (1854).
1874 – A Constitution gives Icelanders control over finances.
End of 19C – Significant emigration to Canada and the US.
1915 – Women given the right to vote.
1918 – Icelandic autonomy under the suzerainty of the king of Denmark.
Second World War – Installation military bases by the Allies.

THE REPUBLIC OF ICELAND

1944 – The republic of Iceland is declared on 17 June.
1949 – The American army establishes a base in Keflavík.
1955 – Halldór Laxness receives the Nobel Prize in Literature.
1960-1976 – Cod Wars between Iceland and Great Britain.
1974 – Route 1 (the Ring Road) is completed.
1980-1996 – Vigdís Finnbogadóttir is elected president. Summit

© Ragnar Th Sigurdsson@arctic-images.com/Promote Iceland

Alþingi - Icelandic Parliament - on National Holiday

between Ronald Reagan and Mikhaïl Gorbatchev in Reykjavík (1986). End of beer prohibition (1989).

2006 – Departure of American troops from former US base.

2008 – The national handball team reaches the finals of the Olympic Games in Beijing. The global financial crisis hits Iceland.

2010 – The ash from the Eyjafjöll volcano paralyzes European skies.

2011-2012 – Trial of participative democracy. Ólafur Ragnar Grímsson is re-elected president for his fifth mandate.

2013 – The Constitution is modified after a consultation with the population, but still not approved by the Parliament , which will welcome this same year the first elected representative of the Pirate Party, Birgitta Jonsdottir.

2016 – The national team reaches the quarter finals in its first Euro tournament (famously beating England).

2018 – For the first time in its history, Iceland participates in the World Cup, in Russia, but doesn't pass the group stage.

Icelandic architecture

FUNCTION FIRST

During Iceland's first centuries, the traditional Norwegian habitat was adapted to the conditions of the island. **Farms** were long occupied by one tenant and composed of a row of single-room homes. Walls were made using stone and peat mud, employed instead of wood, which was in scarce supply: it would have to be imported or gleaned from the beaches and was used only for the frame, which supported the tufa (limestone) roof, built steep snow would run off. Due to the difficulty of heating these spaces, openings were minimized and covered with animal skins. Only a handful of foundations remain of these Viking houses. From the 16C, the use of **driftwood** would become common for building houses and churches, some of which remain today. More modest buildings, used until the start of the 20C, were built **embedded into the rock**, topped with characteristic insulating grassy roofs, making them almost camouflaged by the landscape. They have since become museums, as in Núpsstaður.

Characterized by "this absence of style, full of platitudes, that Icelanders have appropriated" (Árni Þórarinsson), contemporary lodgings have kept the necessary functionality for facing the dramatic **weather conditions**. Today houses are sometimes still constructed in wood and covered in painted corrugated iron. You'll find particularly photogenic examples in Reykjavík around Lake Tjörnin; on an inclement day, listen for the pretty sound of the rain hitting the metal. In the vast suburbs outside of the capital, you'll find solid, earthquake-resistant homes encroaching on the lava fields. Though they are modest on the outside, inside you'll find **cozy interiors,** well heated by geothermal energy.

SHAPE-SHIFTING CHURCHES AND NEW URBAN LIGHTHOUSES

Iceland is dotted with a number of symbolic buildings linked to the country's emancipation. An early example is the Alþing, constructed of stone and basalt in 1881; then Hotel Borg, which announced Art Deco style in 1930; and later the Hafnarhús (1939), constructed in raw concrete and metal, introducing the modernist movement to the island. Little wooden churches would be succeeded by solid constructions which would transform the city skylines. The white **Hallgrímskirkja** (1940-1986) dominates the capital with its 'basalt organs', which also flank the church of Akureyri, designed by the same architect, **Guðjón Samúelsson**. Perched on a hill in Borgarholtis the egg-shaped church of Kópavogskirkja, its boat-like shape a reference to maritime culture. In the 1950s, Iceland

santir/iStockphoto.com

Turf houses, Núpsstaður

became interested in the functionalism of Finish designer and architect **Alvar Aalto**, who would design the Nordic House in 1968. In 1992, the **Rádhús** (city hall), with its glass, concrete and moss, would playfully blend and contrast with Lake Tjörnin's waters. During the same period, six geothermal reservoirs were topped with a dome to create **Perlan** (the pearl), shining atop the town. With the arrival of funds, cranes and construction sites would inherit the capital. Architects would make use of local materials, mixing lava, concrete and glass to create luxurious villas, seafront buildings, cafés and design hotels, like 101 Hotel. The **port's heritage** was refreshed and the capital would be given its own equivalent of Sydney Opera House, which the whole world would come to associate with the city. This was **Harpa**, an opera house and conference center whose construction, interrupted by the financial crisis fallout, was completed in 2011. The imposing facade designed by artist **Ólafur Elíasson** sparkles with a hypnotising shimmer; the sun, the city lights and the waters of the fjord reflect on its surface. An undeniable architectural triumph

Chefs in search of flavour

Iceland's gastronomic reputation still leaves a little to be desired, but for food enthusiasts there are discoveries to be made chefs' use of simple rustic products and some unexpected ingredients and combinations.

SURF AND TURF

For centuries, Icelanders have been consuming lamb and fish. Traditionally **lamb** (*lambakjöt*) was killed in the autumn during *réttir* (the annual sheep round-up), and then smoked (*hangikjöt*), salted and turned into various cured meat preparations (*slátur*) in provision for winter. Everything is eaten: offal, sometimes conserved in whey (*surmatur*), the head (*svið*), and other parts, which are prepared in stews, soups and black pudding (*blódmor*). Excellent **fish** (*fiskur*), is eaten smoked, marinated, dried (*harðfiskur*) or simply boiled. On menus you'll find meltingly soft halibut (*lúða*), monkfish (*skötuselur*), salmon (*lax*), trout (*silungur*), cod (*þorskur*), haddock (*ýsa*) and herring (*sild*). Fish eggs (*kaviar*) are eaten salted or kept in tubes and spread on bread. Whale (*hvalur*) is mostly exported to Japan, but its red and firm flesh is sometimes featured on particularly Icelandic menus. Shark is generally consumed after being hung (*hákarl*), creating a rather *virile* taste and smell! Finally, perhaps unexpectedly,

grilled or smoked puffin (*lundi*) is a treat not to be missed. **Potato** (*kartafla*) with melted cream and butter is the supreme accompaniment to these dishes. Food is also often served with a range of **breads**: rye bread (*hverabrauð*), lightly sugared black bread (*rúgbrauð*) and a kind of savoury pancake (*flatbrauð*). Every now and again, **Þorrametur** events or "Viking banquets" are held, bringing together all these dishes.

A great deal of **dairy products** are also consumed: try yogurt varieties **skyr** and *súrmjólk* accompanied by rhubarb and bay jam. *Skyr* enriches pancakes (*pönnukökur*), cakes (notably the delicious *skyr* cheesecake) and doughnuts; it can even accompany bananas heated under geothermal-powered greenhouses for an undeniably Icelandic dessert! Icelandic brands such as Opal, Sirius, Nóa and Lindú, produce a variety of sweets, often flavored with local favorite liquorice (*lakkrís*). In terms of **drinks**, the national treasure is named **brennivín**, a schnapps flavored with caraway. Icelanders are also the world's fourth biggest consumers of coffee!

FAST FOOD AND NEW WAVE

The very popular **pýlsur** (Icelandic hot dog), as well as pizzas and burgers have for some decades now

Drying fish

occupied the freezers and stomachs of Icelanders. This is all washed down by a generous helping of fizzy drinks, including the florescent local special, Egils Appelsin.

However, things are evolving, and alongside canned foods *(niðursoðinn matur)*, supermarkets have solid fruit and vegetable aisles, as well as *bakarí* stocked with choice pastries and breads.

Thanks to the country's young chefs, a **nouvelle cuisine** was born at the end of the 90s. Inspired by their own island and their experiences abroad, they employed fresh, traditional produce and blended and prepared them with a decidedly more contemporary touch.

At a corresponding price, diners can savor reinvented soups and stews, as well as fish, snow partridges, reindeer and mountain lamb, whose meat is naturally flavored with the wild herbs it feeds on.

Among the reputed chefs of this cuisine, you'll find **Gunnar Karl Gíslason** and**Hákon Már Örvarsson**, who has been awarded a Bocuse de bronze.

Maps

Inside

Cover

Photo credits

Page 4

Gullfoss: © tobiasjo/iStockphoto.com
Harpa: © Ragnar Th Sigurdsson@arctic-images.com/Promote Iceland
Seltún: © VvoeVale/iStockphoto.com
National Museum of Iceland in Reykjavík: © Danuta Hyniewska/age fotostock
Blue Lagoon: © Anne-Marie et Michel Detay/Michelin

Page 5

Þingvellir National Park: © Ragnar Th. Sigurdsson/age fotostock
Hallgímskirkja: © Fly_dragonfly/iStockphoto.com
Lake Kleifarvatn: © narloch-liberra/iStockphoto.com
Geysir: © franckreporter/iStockphoto.com
Krýsuvíkurberg: © mmac72/iStockphoto.com

- Charleston
- London
- Milan Bergamo & the Lakes
- New Orleans
- New York
- Paris
- Reykjavik

Visit your preferred bookseller for the short-stay series, plus Michelin's comprehensive range of Green Guides, maps, and famous red-cover Hotel and Restaurant guides.

124

The**Green**Guide short-stays **Reykjavik**

Editorial Director	Cynthia Ochterbeck
Editor	Sophie Friedman
Production Manager	Natasha George
Cartography	Peter Wrenn, Nicolas Breton
Picture Editor	Yoshimi Kanazawa
Interior Design	Laurent Muller
Layout	Natasha George

Contact Us

Michelin Travel and Lifestyle North America
One Parkway South
Greenville, SC 29615
USA
travel.lifestyle@us.michelin.com

Michelin Travel Partner
Hannay House
39 Clarendon Road
Watford, Herts WD17 1JA
UK
✆01923 205240
travelpubsales@uk.michelin.com
www.viamichelin.co.uk

Special Sales

For information regarding bulk sales,
customized editions and premium sales,
please contact us at:
travel.lifestyle@us.michelin.com

YOUR OPINION IS ESSENTIAL
TO IMPROVING OUR PRODUCTS

Help us by answering the
questionnaire on our website:
satisfaction.michelin.com

Michelin Travel Partner

Société par actions simplifiées au capital de 15 044 940 EUR
27 cours de l'Ile Seguin - 92100 Boulogne Billancourt (France)
R.C.S. Nanterre 433 677 721

© Michelin Travel Partner
ISBN 978-2-067239-95-1
Printed: January 2019
Printer: Estimprim